ISLAMIC BANKING

ISLAMIC BANKING
THE NEW DYNAMICS

Edited by
Katuri Nageswara Rao

2012

Icfai Books
The Icfai University Press

ISLAMIC BANKING: THE NEW DYNAMICS

Editor: Katuri Nageswara Rao

First Edition: 2012
Printed in India

Published by

This book is published by IUP.
University Campus, Agartala-Simna Road,
P.O. Kamalghat Sadar, Agartala – 799210, Tripura (West)
E-mail: info@iupindia.org
Website: www.books.iupindia.org

ISBN: 978-81-314-2726-2

Contents

Overview

Islamic banking is faith based banking, based on the principles enunciated by the shariah, essentially targeted for the Muslim population, who account for over 1.7 billion people. However, some of the principles of this type of banking attract non-Muslims as well, though not in good numbers. Islamic banking prohibits payment or receipt of interest. It is ethically well-rooted as it does not allow lending to commercial activities based on vice, like gambling, pornography drinking, smoking, drug trafficking etc. It frowns excessive financial leverage and highly speculative activities.

This book deals with the global prospective of Islamic Banking. It is set in two sections, namely "**Perspectives**" and "**Country/Regional Experiences**".

Section I: Perspectives

"**Islamic Banking – An Overview**" is by *Katuri Nageswara Rao*. Globally, Islamic banking has been growing steadily if not steeply, at a rate of about

10 to 15% every year. In over 51 countries, Islamic financial institutions are in operation, providing Islamic faith-compliant financial products and services, as variants to the conventional ones. However, the biggest challenge is to establish their feasibility and gain regulatory recognition and popularity. The question of sound risk management principles, accounting and auditing standards besides financial reporting standards is very crucial. And so are the attempts to render them Basel-2 compliant.

When a traditional bank decides to fully transform into an Islamic institution it has to ensure that all the assets and liabilities of its balance sheets are non-interest bearing in nature. The assets should be "Murabaha" form (cost plus financing) of contracts. Likewise, its deposits should be Mudarabah form (profit and loss sharing) of contracts.

The bank could rely on a tawarrug instrument in order to convert an existing loan (bearing interest) into an Islam compatible instrument. A tawarrug is a contract whereby a customer requests a bank to acquire a specific commodity (e.g., metal or wool) on his behalf. The customer will repay the bank the cost of the commodity plus an agreed margin in installments. The customer then requests the bank to sell the commodity right away in the commodity spot market. Hence, through this transaction, the customer obtains immediate financing (via the spot sale of the commodity) which will be repaid later (via installment payments to the bank).

Likewise, Diminishing Musharakah is yet another variant of Islamic banking. It is relatively of recent origin. Under this financing mode, a banker and the borrower partake jointly to acquire the ownership of an equipment or property or even a joint commercial enterprise. The bank segments its share into a number of units with the premise that the borrower buys these units periodically, one by one. This way, the borrower increases his share of units while the banker decreases his units. Ultimately, all the units are purchased by the borrower and he becomes the sole owner of the asset or business in question.

Similarly, I jara-wa-Iqtina is a novel way of offering the Islamic version of leasing, renting or hiring. Under this method, the banker finances the asset (movable or immovable) and the borrower agrees to pay a prefixed rental or to buy the asset. The rental installment is suitably fixed so that the financing bank gets back not only the principle amount loaned but also some predefined profit.

A Mudaraba form of Islamic financing typically represents the spirit behind this faith-based lending. It is an agreement between the bank and the borrower. The borrower's duty is to provide managerial and entrepreneurial skill for the business, while the bank agrees to fund the venture. Of course the business, which could be a trade, service or a manufacturing industry, aims at earning profit. The profit or loss thus earned is shared in a prefixed proportion between the bank and the borrower. This way, the practice of charging interest on the loan by the bank is not followed as it is construed as an unislamic practice, but the bank shares both profits losses. In fact it carries in the process, higher credit risk.

Musharaka is a near approximation of a joint venture. Under this, the borrower and the banker contribute in a prefixed ratio, to the equity capital of a joint venture, which is expected to be a short-term venture. They also divide the profits or losses in a prefixed ratio, not necessarily in the ratio of contributions of the equity capital.

With regards to insurance products in place of the conventional non-mutual insurance, which is not a Shari 'ah compliant product, 'Takaful' can be substituted. Takaful is based on the concept of mutuality among insured parties, as in conventional mutual insurance. That is, several individuals agree to pool resources with the understanding that in case of need, each of them is entitled to draw resources from the pool.

Over a period of time, there could be Sukuks (bonds) and even financial derivative investment that are Shari 'ah compliant.

Islamic banking, therefore, offers, a relatively more superior and ethically more correct banking for the purists, even though in implementation, there are challenges, which in any case, are not insurmountable. This banking model in essence, encourages partnerships of the entrepreneurs with the bank (Musharakah).

The subsequent article **"Islamic Banking: Can you Afford to Ignore it?"** is by *Vincent Chin, Knut Storholm, Sven-Olaf Vathje, Nor Azah Razali* and *Mohammmed Badi.* Islamic banking - banking that adheres to the tenets of Sharia (or Islamic law) – is a rapidly growing niche in financial services. Holding natural appeal for followers of the Islamic faith, who constitute roughly 25% of the world's population, Islamic banking products are also attracting increasing interest from many non-Muslims. Banks that are global in scope, or that aspire to be, should take note of this trend.

Pure Islamic banks, along with Islamic subsidiaries and "windows" of conventional banks, currently control close to $400 billion in assets globally, compared with $100 billion in assets in 2000. Since Sharia forbids the earning of riba (interest) depositors are treated like equity shareholders. They earn a portion of the bank's profits instead of interest. Loans are structured as asset-based diminishing-partnership or leasing agreements. A sukuk, or Islamic bond, is asset-based rather than debt-based, with bondholders receiving "rent" on the asset instead of interest. Overall, a premium is put on the concepts of transparency, cooperative ventures, shared risk and contractual certainty—elements that loom larger than ever before in the wake of such events as the subprime crisis and other headline-grabbing scandals that have challenged public confidence in financial institutions.

Sharia also prohibits financial involvement in industries such as those related to gambling, alcohol and adult media, hence Islamic banking products are of interest to the burgeoning ethical-investing segment.

There are essentially three kinds of Islamic banking players: pure Islamic banks that offer only Sharia-compliant products; fully Islamic divisions or subsidiaries of conventional banks and so-called Islamic windows of conventional banks, where Sharia-compliant products are sold alongside traditional offerings. Regulation adds a further layer of complexity to the landscape. Sharia boards—groups of Islamic scholars that make decisions on regional, national or bank-by-bank level regarding which products and practices are permitted—function as de facto regulatory bodies.

Islamic banking is also growing in such global financial centers as London, Zurich and Hong Kong. In the United Kingdom, investment-banking and asset-management products have thus far been the most prominent offerings.

In other financial centers such as Zurich and Geneva, the current focus is on leveraging deep and long-term relationships with wealthy Muslim clients from the Middle East who are seeking Islamic private-banking services. In Asia, Hong Kong's position as a gateway to China is attracting Middle Eastern institutions wishing to invest petrodollars in China through Sharia-compliant vehicles.

The fact that many banks, especially in the Middle East, are short on manufacturing capabilities to develop attractive Islamic products prevents them from absorbing inexpensive excess liquidity in the market. Long-term winners will be those banks that dedicate sufficient resources to structuring the most innovative Sharia-compliant products and that tailor those products to specific markets and segments.

The Islamic banking industry needs common and internationally accepted standards on capital adequacy, risk, and asset-quality assessment.

The article **"Islamic Financing Arrangements used in Islamic Banking"** by *Ehsan Zarrokh* discusses the broad features of a strategy which holds the promise of successfully implementing an Islamic system of finance. The features are as follows:

- The process has to be guided by basic legislative efforts covering all the essential elements of the proposed programme.
- The legislation would define riba (interest) and prohibit transactions connected with it.
- The application of the law would be unqualified and without exception, thus the entire financial sector, covering banking, government finance and foreign transactions would be covered in its ambit.
- Given the unqualified and non-exceptional nature of the proposed law, even existing relations will have to be converted into permissible forms, for which a suitable time frame, within a phasing-in period, will be allowed.

- The law should also provide for the constitution of a Shari 'ah Board which would assist the SBP to formulate permissible means of financing. Such means, specified with the prior approval of the Board, will only be illustrative and no restrictions will be placed on banks and financial institutions to design means of financing which are free of riba.
- A major portion of the law will have to be devoted to a plan of restructuring the fiscal policy which comprises a scheme for the privatization of public sector assets and the use of its proceeds for the settlement of the outstanding stock of public debt.

The proposed strategy is based on the clear recognition of the scope implied by the prohibition of riba. This is critical, for otherwise the solution will continue to elude us.

"Islamic Banking and Finance: Shari 'a-Compliance and the Reinterpretation of Riba" is written by *Sapana Shah*. The growth of Islamic banking is symptomatic of the global demand of Shari 'a-compliant products. This growth illustrates not only the desire to follow the religious mandates and the spirit of Islam, but also the socio-economic capabilities of such a popular system as well. The current tools are inadequate to fulfill such desires and expectations and provide some difficulty in becoming compatible with the Western banking system. The only solution would be to provide a moderate form of interest. As a matter of Islamic law, this could only be achieved by a second consensus to change the prevailing interpretation of riba. While some countries do endorse alternative views, as opposed to the classical view, a second consensus will render a uniform agreement of the boundaries of riba and provide a powerful movement towards a more equitable distribution of wealth.

Islamic banking prohibits 'trading in risk' or 'risk taking' (Gharar). The issue of Gharar is traditionally overcome when the parties to a contract have adequate knowledge of the subject matter of the transaction and the counter-values they intend to exchange.

Islamic and Western banking methods fundamentally differ. This is not to say that they are incompatible, but rather that the incentives for profit are for different purposes and goals.

Mudaraba is a profit-and-loss sharing financial system, which is equivalent to venture capitalism. In this type of transaction, an investor trusts an entrepreneur with capital; if the entrepreneur makes a profit, he would agree to share a certain percentage with the investor. If there are any losses of capital, only the investor bears them. Mudaraba is one of the most basic forms of Islamic banking.

Musharaka is a capitalistic partnership agreement whereby investors contribute capital together, sharing the losses and profits on an agreed-upon equation. In this arrangement, clearly without the use of riba, the losses and profits are shared among the participants. Like mudaraba, musharaka is also one of the most basic forms of Islamic banking.

Murabaha constitutes financing on a "cost plus" basis. Here, the bank purchases goods at a certain price and resells it to customers at a higher price. Under traditional banking, the customer is likely to incur fees or interest calculations if there is a default. Under murabaha, the customer is only liable for the contracted good.

Bai'muajjal this is an investment activity tool is equivalent to a deferred payment financing. Here, the financial institution purchases the contract for property or goods on a deferred payment schedule and then resells the property or goods to the customer. The financial institution pays the supplier on a progressive schedule, and the customer pays the institution through installments on the progressive schedule. Here as well it appears that the financial institution interposes a form of riba; however, since the nature of the transaction is trading rather than lending, the reselling at a higher price is justified.

Ijara is a lease transaction in which the financial institution purchases goods, usually machinery or equipment, and leases it to the customer. The customer would pay the institution a rental fee for a set period; if the customer wishes to purchase the good before or after the period, he may do so.

Bai' salam is a transaction in which the entrepreneur sells his goods to a bank at a price determined in advance of delivery. Therefore, the bank sells the goods to the customer at a price determined during the formation of the contract, and the goods are delivered at a later date.

The subsequent article "**Banking for the Poor: The Role of Islamic Banking in Microfinance Initiatives**" writtten by *Asyraf Wajdi Dusuki* states that microfinance requires innovative approaches beyond the traditional financial intermediary role. Among others, building human capacity through social intermediation and designing group-based lending programmes are proven to be among the effective tools to reduce transaction costs and lower exposure to numerous financial risks in relation to providing credit to the rural poor. This paper also suggests the use of special purpose vehicle (SPV) as one of the possible alternatives for Islamic banks channelling funds to the poor.

Islamic banks may benefit from a spectrum of Shariah-compliant sources of funds and offer a wide array of financing instruments catering to different needs and demands of their clients. Furthermore, the use of a bankruptcy-remote entity like SPV can protect Islamic banks from any adverse effect of microfinance activities.

Concern over credit provision and finance accessibility for the poor via microfinance is also relevant to Islamic banks. The banks should shoulder greater social welfare responsibilities and religious commitments to achieve the Islamic economic objectives, including social justice, equitable distribution of income and wealth and promoting economic development.

Conventional microfinance relies heavily on simple interest-based deposits, government subsidies, donations and loans. On the other hand, Islamic microfinance can benefit from a wide array of instruments for funds mobilization. Islamic microfinance instruments may be broadly divided into: (1) Internal Resources and (2) External Resources. The former relates to financial resources that can be mobilized internally to ensure self-sustainability and self-sufficiency, while the latter reflects the common practice of microfinance institutions worldwide which rely on external parties to provide financial resources like government grants, subsidies and donations.

Microfinance requires innovative approaches beyond the traditional financial intermediary role. Among others, building human capacity through social intermediation and designing group-based lending programmes are proven to be among the effective tools to reduce transaction costs and lower exposure to numerous financial risks in relation to providing credit to the rural poor group-based approach also fosters a better flow of information between lenders and borrowers and hence results in less adverse selection and moral hazard in the credit market.

The article "**Ethical Money: Financial Growth in the Muslim World**" is authored by *Bjorn Sorenson*. Current financial crises, such as the bursting of the housing bubble in the United States and the accompanying credit crunch, highlight the need for greater moral inquiry into the structure of financial regulation. The development of Socially Responsible Investing and the proliferation of Shariah-compliant finance bring much-needed ethical scrutiny to financial investments. As the Islamic financial services industry develops, it faces obstacles in creating new Shariah products, developing common practices to approve such products and serving niche and retail consumers. New legal customs and new legal scholarship provide lawyers a unique opportunity for the development of transnational business practices, the examination of the ethics of finance, and the chance to participate in substantive dialogue about morality in a globalizing world.

Islamic finance is based on an understanding of economic justice. Prohibitions against riba or interest, must be considered in a moral framework. Additionally, Islam prohibits excessive gharar (uncertainty) and maisir (gambling).

Although the Islamic financial services industry as a whole is growing at record pace, two factors inhibit accelerated expansion. First, the creation of Shariah-compliant financial products is a time consuming process because of the unique structures and rigorous approval process. Secondly, it remains difficult to get Shariah-compliant financial products and services to ordinary consumers around the globe.

Islamic finance needs to reach out to the poor, defining them as customers with profitable needs rather than an indigent and commercially nonexistent market segment.

Section II: Country/Regional Experiences

"Sri Lanka and the Scope for Islamic Banking" is by *Faizal Salieh*. Sri Lanka is one of the few non-Islamic countries to have legislated for Islamic banking. The revised Banking Act No 30 of 1988, as amended in 2005, allows both commercial banks and specialized banks to operate on a Shariah-compliant basis. The regulators are responding to the growing Islamic market segment, both local and global, and the global developments and trends in Islamic banking. Islamic bankers and Shariah scholars are scarce resources and critical success factors for the industry's future growth and development.

Following the new legislation, some of the existing conventional banks are expected to open Islamic banking windows with a view to preventing their Muslim customers from migrating to Islamic banks. It is also possible that the market might see a few new entrants to Islamic banking, although the Central Bank has upped the minimum capital requirements for licensing substantially.

The size of the Islamic market is estimated at around US$500 million-US$600 million. Relevant changes to the fiscal and legislative environments will soon be necessary to facilitate Islamic banking transactions.

Yet another challenge facing the industry is the competency gap in human resources, both at the regulatory and market levels.

The next article **"Settlement of Islamic Banking Disputes in Indonesia: Opportunities and Challenges"** is written by *Abdul Rasyid*. The growth of Islamic banking in Indonesia has been progressing steadily and swiftly. Presently there are 3 full-fledged Islamic banks, 19 Shariah business units and 92 Shariah Rural Banks.

This paper analyzes the challenges faced by Basyarnas as a non-litigation forum and religious courts as litigation institutions both of which have been conferred with the competency to settle disputes in the area of Islamic banking.

The dispute settlement of Islamic banking in the mode of alternative dispute resolution, through Basyarnas, has some advantages, which may be identified as follows:

- It reposes trust in the parties by placing the dispute settlement in their hands so that they may use this trust in a respectful and responsible manner.
- The parties place their trust in the arbiter with full confidence that the dispute will be resolved by a person who has the expertise in the field.
- The process of taking decision through Basyarnas is expeditious, less complicated and inexpensive.
- As the parties entrust their dispute in voluntary manner for settlement to the trusted person, it naturally implies they have agreed to implement the decision given by the arbiter, as it is the natural outcome of their own agreement in appointing the arbiter. An agreement implies a promise and promises are to be fulfilled.
- Islamic arbitration process contains reconciliation as its integral component; hence it becomes part of the Basyarnas process.
- A clear inference which may be drawn from Basyarnas process is that Islamic law is to be used as the basic principle in settling disputes in the area of Islamic banking.

Looking at the impressive improvement of the Islamic banks in Indonesia, the existence of Basyarnas and religious court as institutions which have the authority to settle the disputes of Islamic banking is very impressive. Basyarnas as a non-litigation institution can play an important role in resolving disputes of Islamic banking expeditiously, inexpensively and simply. Its process of reconciliation is indeed attractive to the disputing parties. However, it remains to be seen how it is managed in a professional manner.

"Islamic Banks in Jordan: Performance and Efficiency Analysis" is by *Ali Salman Saleh* and *Rami Zeitun*. Islamic banking commenced in Jordan approximately two decades ago. Ever since it has played an important role in financing and contributes to different economic and social sectors in the country. This paper, therefore, examines and analyzes the Jordanian experience of Islamic banking, focusing on the two largest Islamic banks in the country: the Jordan Islamic Bank for Finance and Investment (JIBFI) and the Islamic International Arab Bank (IIAB), and evaluates these Islamic banks' performance. The paper also sheds some light on the domestic and global challenges that this sector faces. The authors used a performance evaluation methodology and conducted profit maximization, capital structure and liquidity tests, and found that both banks' efficiency and ability has increased, they have expanded their investment and activities and played an important role in financing projects in Jordan. Another interesting finding is that these banks focused on short-term investments, which is often found in most Islamic banking practices. The research also found that Islamic banks have a high growth in credit facilities and in profitability; and postulates whether this might encourage other banks to adopt the Islamic financial system.

By using performance evaluation procedures, which are important to measure the growth and development of any bank, this paper found that both the IIAB and JIBFI banks efficiency and the profitability increased. Both banks expanded their investments and activities and have played significant roles in financing important projects in the market. These Islamic banks had a high growth in credit facilities and profitability.

Additional interesting findings were that these Islamic banks have focused on short- rather than long-term investments. This seems to be the case for most Islamic banking practices where the capital structure becomes stronger and depends on short-term investment. In comparing the two banks, the authors found that the Jordan Islamic Bank for Finance and Investment has increased its lending activities more than the Islamic International Arab Bank, and the facilities of the latter have grown at a higher rate. The results also show that the Jordan Islamic Bank for Finance and Investment has a high profitability, which should encourage other banks to employ financial Islamic products.

The paper sheds some light on the development of Islamic banking globally. This sector has not only grown in the Muslim world, but has also gained significant attention in the Western world, with over 250 Islamic banks worldwide controlling approximately US$400 billion in assets and client money. The growth of these banks is proof of their success, and an indication that these banks continue to grow in number and size worldwide.

Islamic banks in Jordan are facing many challenges like conflicts in the region, the economic slowdown, globalization, increased cash surpluses with limited finance and investment opportunities, public awareness and acceptance, lack of institutions that conduct research and development in this area, lack of skilled and professional people and local competition from large numbers of commercial banks that are operating in the country.

The article **"Funding and Financing in Islamic Banking System"** by *Achmad Tohirin* and *Abdul Ghafar Ismail* aims to analyze the relation between deposit and financing sides of Islamic banking industry in Malaysia. The Granger causality test has been applied to examine the causality between deposit and financing. The results show that unidirectional relationship between deposit and financing exists. However, the result also shows that the directional relationship change when the test uses different lags.

In discussing the relation between deposits and financing in Islamic bank, this paper has proved the unidirectional causal relationship. However, it has not been able to explore more information concerning the causality relationship especially for mudarabah deposit and mudarabah financing due to the unavailability of the data with the required classification.

"Risk Management: Islamic Financial Policies – Islamic Banking and its Potential Impact" is authored by *Thomas A Timberg*. Though Bank Muamalat and the BPRS offer a full range of Islamic deposit and credit products, most Islamic credit in Indonesia has taken the form of trade finance (bai al salaam, bai bitsama ajil, istishna or murabaha), though the proportion declines as the partnership or trust provision of working capital (musyarakat and mudharabah) increases. Rates (charged and paid) differ considerably between institutions and from time to time, but the average rates on Islamic credit often approximate those of other institutions.

Although Bank Muamalat did not suffer as severely as many large banks from the financial crisis, it did require some management change and has begun healthy growth again. Bank Perkreditan Rakyat Sharish and Bait Maal Wat Tamwil (BPRS and BMT) have been growing despite the monetary crisis.

The BMT have mobilized a great deal of savings and provided financial services to large constituencies, many of whom have never been served before. They have a large prospective market and the advantage of building on the informal network created by the Islamic institutions with which they are associated as well as the moral sanction that comes with that affiliation. However, as largely unsupervised and unguaranteed institutions, many of which are run by relatively inexperienced personnel using new methodologies, they clearly present prudential dangers—though not different in principle from those posed by all savings and loan cooperatives in Indonesia.

In form rather than substance Islamic finance is quite similar to other finances. Many of its instruments are the same as those used by other financial institutions—leasing, advance purchase etc. Its difference lies in the social impulse for sharing—responsibility, risk and property. Consequently, fixed-interest transactions in which risk is assigned entirely to the borrower are avoided. More importantly for participants Islamic finance represents part of a divinely sanctioned economic gestalt into which they fit.

Thus Islamic finance

- Enables financial services to an otherwise underserved group including small, rural and agricultural producer;

- Furthers a social thrust to assist smaller producers and consumers and is often given in the context of a movement to assist them;
- Requires some adjustment, mostly formal, of techniques and regulation to take account of Islamic values.

Islamic finance, as part of a financial sector development strategy, ought to be encouraged, mainstreamed and adjusted to. An IMF study on the matter concludes that Islamic finance should be encouraged by regulation and supervision that accommodate its forms while ensuring that clients' unfamiliarity with it is not exploited to defraud them. Normal prudential and supervision norms should be adequate. The IMF study does, however, suggest that higher capital adequacy ratios and more detailed disclosure requirements may be appropriate. The paper suggests a modified CAMEL (capital adequacy, asset quality, management, earnings, liquidity) system of banking supervision for Islamic banking. Special risks are the generally uncollateralized nature of Islamic banking and greater risks in the profit-sharing forms of lending. To the extent that Islamic banking is collateralized or does not engage in profit-sharing forms, the issues are less serious. Nonetheless, the Islamic banks are often more comfortable with specialized regulations and infrastructure that recognize their peculiarities. The BMT in particular, need adequate supervision and some guarantee for their depositors, though not as elaborate as those provided to commercial banks and BPRs.

Islamic banking should be mainstreamed by maximizing the interaction between Islamic institutions and the rest of the financial system, subject to the constraints of shariah. The financial system and its regulation should be adjusted as necessary to accommodate the other two thrusts.

Donors should ensure that their assistance to financial system development includes Islamic financial institutions. This will help include otherwise excluded groups and avoid regulatory loopholes.

Section I

Perspectives

1

Islamic Banking – An Overview

Katuri Nageswara Rao

Islamic banking professes ethical principles in lending and prohibits payment and receipt of interest as it misallocates resources and results in created money and inflation. It favors collective endeavors of entrepreneurs, with banks acting as partners. It roots for financing small borrowers. The question is how to customize existing banking, insurance and investment products into Shariah's compliant ones.

Conventional banking involves securing deposits in driblets from savers for the purpose of lending or investing. This is essentially an intermediation function where bankable propositions are financed and investments are made either in safe treasury bonds or corporate papers of varying qualities. Banking, principally a service activity, has profit motive as a commercial organization. Conventional banking thrives on public trust, with highly leveraged positions involving about eight percent as net worth and as high as 92 percent of public money. It is precisely for this reason of exceptionally high leverage that banks are regulated very closely by Central bankers to protect the interests of the depositors in particular. The regulators expect banks to conduct its functions on sound commercial lines, following efficient risk management principles and complying with what are called prudential norms.

Islamic banking, on the other hand, is faith based banking, based on the principles enunciated by the Shariah, essentially targeted for the Muslim population, who account for over 1.7bn. people. However, some of the principles of this type of banking attract non-Muslims as well, though not in good numbers. Islamic banking prohibits payment or receipt of interest. It does not allow lending to commercial activities based on vice, like gambling, pornography drinking, smoking, drug trafficking etc. So, it is ethically well rooted. It frowns excessive financial leverage and highly speculative activities.

Globally, Islamic banking has been growing steadily, if not steeply, at a rate of about 10 to 15 percent per year. In over 51 countries, Islamic financial institutions are in operation, providing Islamic faith compliant financial products and services, as variants to the conventional ones. However, the biggest challenge is to establish their feasibility, gain regulatory recognition and popularity. The question of sound risk management principles, accounting and auditing standards besides financial reporting standards are very crucial. So are the attempts to render them Basel-2 compliant.

Faith Based Financing

Islamic banking aims at offering bankable products and services, as variants of the traditional ones, which are Sharia-compliant. Often, it is the community of Islamic scholars who sits on judgment on this issue. They work in co-ordination with lawyers and bankers. However, this process results in different interpretations in different regions, often leading to the creation of non-uniform products, sometimes the distinctions created between Islamic banking products and traditional ones look trivial or inconsequential.

There are, however, certain organizations that have been working to bring in the much needed uniformity. The National Sharia Board of Malaysia is one such. Its functions include acting as an authoritative body to advise the nation on Islamic banking. It co-ordinates Shariah issues with respect to Islamic banking. It analyses and evaluates Shariah aspects for new products/schemes submitted by banks. Similar institutions are there in Kuwait, Indonesia, and Saudi Arabia etc. There are efforts to bring all such institutions into one operational entity. The progress in this direction is rather slow.

Banking on Faith: Sharia-Compliant Assests, 2007, $bn	
	Assets
Iran	154.6
Saudi Arabia	69.4
Malaysia	65.1
Kuwait	37.7
United Arab Emirates	35.4
Brunei	31.5
Bahrain	26.3
Pakistan	15.9
Lebanon	14.3
Britain	10.4
Source: The Banker	

The Accounting and Auditing Organization for Islamic Financial Institutions (AAOIFI), situated in the state of Baharin, is a non-profit autonomous international Islamic institution, that was established in 1991 to look into issues like auditing, accounting, governance and ethical standards for Islamic banking and financial institutions[1]. It conducts professional qualification programs and corporate compliance programs. It has the support of 155 institutional members from 40 countries[2]. The institutions include central banks and Islamic financial institutions worldwide. The standards prescribed by AAOIFI are being adopted in many Islamic nations.

The Islamic Financial Services Board (IFSB) established in the year 2002 in Kaulalampur, Malaysia, IFSB promotes the development of a transparent and prudent Islamic financial services industry through introduction of international standards consistent with Shariah principles[3]. Its functions complement those of the Basel Committee on Banking Supervision, International Organization of Securities Commissions and the International Association of Insurance Supervisors[4]. At present there are 150 members for IFSB, including regulatory and supervisory authorities,

---

1 *www.irtipms.org/OpenSave.asp?pub=222.pdf*

2 *http://goliath.ecnext.com/coms2/gi_0199-7333893/Special-Supplement-Top-500-Islamic.html*

3 *http://www.openpr.com/news/12480/Islamic-Financial-Services-Board-organizing-Islamic-Finance-Challenges-Seminar-in-Tokyo.html*

4 *http://www.iaisweb.org/index.cfm?pageID=49.*

IMF, World Bank, Bank for International Settlements, Islamic Development Bank, Asian Development Bank besides various Islamic banking institutions.

IFSB has so far issued the standards relating to risk management, capital adequacy, corporate governance, supervisory review process, transparency and market discipline, recognition of ratings on Shariah-compliant financial instruments and development of Islamic money markets[5]. It is in the process of issuing further standards and guidelines in areas like capital adequacy, exposure draft, and corporate governance for Insurance sector (takaful operations), Shariah governance and market conduct.

Islamic Fiqh Academy Established in the year 1998 in Jeddah (Saudi Arabia); IFA is a subsidiary organ of the organization of the Islamic conference[6]. Its members are selected from the best scholars of the Islamic world from different fields. It is also involved in issuing Zakats on various issues like corporate funds, currencies, debts, assets, leased properties, salaries, wages and investments etc., which have relevance for Islamic banking and finance. These Zakats are generally respected by Islamic finance practitioners and policy markers.

International Monetary Fund (IMF), in its June 2007 working paper, titled, "Introducing Islamic Banks into Conventional Banking System", discusses certain challenges facing Islamic banks, relating to segregation of funds, setting up Islamic windows, Islamic Investment banking, licensing of Islamic banks, etc. It also deals with issues relating to the introduction of non-bank Islamic financial institutions, and instruments, prudential supervision, etc.

With regards to segregation of funds, the working paper observes that the funds intended for Shariah-compatible investment should not be mixed with those of non-Islamic investments to ensure purity of transactions[7]. It recommends that "conventional banks wishing to offer Islamic products must guarantee and publicize that mix-up of funds does not happen. This way, when a conventional bank opens an Islamic window, it is in fact establishing a separate entity with a different capital fund, accounts and reporting systems." As the activities of the Islamic window expands, the bank many consider

[5] *www.assaif.org/content/download/584/4385/file/MDYs%20SukukShariah.pdf*

[6] *http://alimdotcom.blogspot.com/2008_01_13_archive.html*

[7] *http://www.imf.org/external/pubs/ft/survey/so/2007/RES0919A.htm*

fully segregating the window into a separate subsidiary[8]. The subsidiary may over a period of time become a full fledged bank opines the working paper.

Islamic investment banking has also been taking firm roots through Islamic compliant investment instruments like Sovereign Sukuks (sovereign bonds), Corporate Sukuks (corporate bonds), investments vehicles (hedge funds) etc. The working paper notes that the petro dollar funds of the gulf nations could be a good source to transform into the aforesaid Islamic investment products.

When a traditional bank decides to fully transform into an Islamic institution, it has to ensure that all the assets and liabilities of its balance sheets should be non-interest bearing in nature. Its assets, therefore, should be in Murabaha form (cost plus financing) contracts. Likewise, its deposits should be in Mudarabah form (profit and loss sharing) contracts.

The bank could rely on a *tawarrug* instrument in order to convert an existing loan (bearing interest) into an Islam compatible instrument. A *tawarrug* is a contract whereby a customer requests a bank to acquire a specific commodity (e.g. metal or wool) on his behalf. The customer will repay the bank the cost of the commodity plus an agreed margin in installments. The customer then requests the bank to sell the commodity right away in the commodity spot market. Hence, through this transaction, the customer can obtain immediate financing (via the spot sale of the commodity) which will be repaid at later dates (via the installment payments to the bank)[9].

Likewise, Diminishing Musharakah is yet another variant of Islamic banking. This is relatively of recent origin. Under this financing mode, a banker and the borrower partake jointly to acquire the ownership of an equipment or property or even a joint commercial enterprise. The bank segments its share into a number of units with the premise that the borrower buys these units periodically, one by one. This way, the borrower increases his share of units while the banker decreases his units. Ultimately all the units are purchased by the borrower and hence he becomes the sole owner of the asset or business in question.

---

8 *http://www.scribd.com/doc/7794714/Introducing-Islamic-Bank-Into-Conventional-Bank-IMF-Working-Paper*

9 Ibid.

Similarly Ijara-wa-Iqtina is a novel way of offering Islamic version of leasing, renting or hiring. Under this method, the banker finances the asset (movable or immovable) and the borrower agrees to pay a prefixed rental undertakes to buy the asset. The rental installment is suitably fixed so that the financing bank gets back not only the principle amount loaned but also some predefined profit.

A Modaraba form of Islamic financing typically represents the spirit behind this faith-based lending. It is an agreement between the bank and the borrower. The borrower's duty is to provide managerial and entrepreneurial skill for the business, while the bank agrees to fund the venture. Of course the business, which could be a trade, service or a manufacturing industry, aims at earning profit. The profit or loss thus earned is shared in a prefixed proportion between the bank and the borrower. This way, the practice of charging interest on the loan by the bank is not followed as it is construed as an un-islamic practice, but bank shares both in profits or losses. In fact it carries in the process, higher credit risk.

Musharika is a near approximation of a joint venture. Under this, the borrower and the banker contribute in a prefixed ratio, to the equity capital of a joint venture, which is expected to be a short-term venture. They also divide the profits or losses in a prefixed ratio, not necessarily in the ratio of contributions of the equity capital.

With regards to insurance products, the working paper notes that in place of the conventional non-mutual insurance, which is not a Shariah's compliant product, 'Takaful' can be substituted, takaful is based on the concept of mutuality among insured parties, as in conventional mutual insurance. That is, several individuals agree to pool resources with the understanding that in case of need, each of them is entitled to draw resources from the pool[10].

The working paper also observes that over a period of time, there could be Sukuks (bonds) and even financial derivative investment that are Shariah's compliant.

There is a thorny issue even with the allocation of capital by the parent bank either to the subsidiary or the separate Islamic bank; as such capital may not have its origin in Islamic compliant sources. A recommended solution is to create an entirely new Islamic Institution, committed to making in future, charitable donations.

---

[10] *http://www.imf.org/external/pubs/ft/wp/2007/wp07175.pdf*

Islamic Banking and Economic Development

Emerging economies depend on the role of banks for inclusive equitable distribution of wealth. That is why these economies accord a place of primacy for banking. Banks on their part are expected to be involved in social and development banking to some extent, preserving at the same time, their profit motive. They also are expected to stick to the basics of prudential lending, namely, end-use principle, purpose orientation, rationing of credit amongst competing claimants etc. But this type of banking does not profess ethical principles in lending or investing, the way Islamic banking does. Also, the recent global financial turbulence has been essentially attributed to very high leverage, very high greed and speculation; which are anathema for Islamic banking. Islam favors collective production through participative efforts and higher level of consumption rather than lavish spending. It prohibits receipt and payment of interest as it misallocates resources and results in created money and inflation. It criticizes conventional banking for its failure to finance the poor with a bankable scheme, due to excessive reliance on security and solvency of the borrower. Viewed from this perspective, perhaps analysts who pitch for popularizing Islamic banking are right in their own way.

Islamic banking, therefore, offers, a relatively more superior and ethically more correct banking for the purists, even though in implementation, there are challenges, which in any case, are not insurmountable. This banking model, in essence, encourages partnerships of the entrepreneurs with the bank (Musharakah).

The Indian Context

India is the second largest Muslim population group in the world but the Islamic banking here, has not taken roots yet. Some financial analysts like Dr. Raghuramarajan, who submitted a report during 2007 to India Planning Commission on Financial Sector Reforms has recommended opening the gates for Islamic banking, to facilitate inflow of more funds especially from the gulf region into Shariah's compliant investment products. Perhaps the government and Reserve Bank could be examining this recommendation seriously.

(Katuri Nageswara Rao is Associate Dean at Icfai School of Financial Studies. He can be reached at nrkaturi@icfaipress.org).

2

Islamic Banking
Can you Afford to Ignore it?

Vincent Chin Knut, Storholm, Sven-Olaf Vathje,
Nor Azah Razali and Mohammed Badi

Islamic banking is one of the fastest-growing segments in financial services, and opportunity abounds. Islamic banking's focus on transparency, cooperative ventures, shared risk, and ethical investing attracts a wide range of both Muslims and non-Muslims alike. Regional markets such as the Middle East and Southeast Asia have varying dynamics that must be understood by banks trying to build a position. The Islamic Banking business is still relatively young, and early movers will have a distinct advantage.

Islamic banking—banking that adheres to the tenets of Sharia (or Islamic law)—is a rapidly growing niche in financial services. Holding natural appeal for followers of the Islamic faith, who constitute roughly 25 percent of the world's population, Islamic banking products are also attracting increasing interest from many non-Muslims. Banks that are global in scope, or that aspire to be, should take note of this trend.

Pure Islamic banks, along with Islamic subsidiaries and "windows" of conventional banks, currently control close to $400 billion in assets globally, compared with $100 billion in assets in 2000.[1] Expansion over the past few years has been driven by high oil prices, which have led to more petrodollar wealth in the Middle East, as well as by an increasing percentage of both Muslims and non-Muslims who find the philosophy of Islamic banking attractive. For example, since Sharia forbids the earning of *riba* (directly translated as *excess,* but often interpreted as *interest*) on the grounds that money generating more money without accompanying liability or risk is detrimental to society, depositors are treated like equity shareholders. They earn a portion of the bank's profits instead of interest. Loans are structured as asset-based diminishing-partnership or leasing agreements. A *sukuk,* or Islamic bond, is asset based rather than debt based, with bondholders receiving "rent" on the asset instead of interest. Overall, a premium is put on the concepts of transparency, cooperative ventures, shared risk, and contractual certainty—elements that loom larger than ever in the wake of such events as the subprime crisis and other headline-grabbing scandals that have challenged public confidence in financial institutions.

Sharia also prohibits financial involvement in industries such as those related to gambling, alcohol, and adult media, so Islamic banking products are of interest to the burgeoning ethical-investing segment. Indeed, many pundits say that Islamic banking, given its attractive characteristics, would quickly become a powerful phenomenon were it called by a secular name. In our view, it may still become a global force if current growth trends gain momentum. The untapped potential is truly vast. Major banks should therefore ask themselves a critical question: given the appeal of Islamic banking both to members of the rapidly growing Muslim faith—already 1.6 billion strong—and to non-Muslims alike, can the opportunity to pursue this business really be ignored?

A Regional Kaleidoscope

There are essentially three kinds of Islamic banking plays: pure Islamic banks that offer only Sharia-compliant products; fully Islamic divisions or subsidiaries of conventional banks; and so-called Islamic windows of conventional banks, where Sharia-compliant products are sold alongside traditional offerings. Regulation adds a

[1] This figure refers to banking assets only, not assets related to Islamic insurance or other financial products that are more difficult to quantify.

further layer of complexity to the landscape. Sharia boards—groups of Islamic scholars that make decisions on a regional, national, or bank-by-bank level regarding which products and practices are permitted—function as de facto regulatory bodies.

Since both customer behavior and regulation vary widely by market, major banks wishing to explore building a position in Islamic banking should take a regional perspective. Let's explore several key markets more closely—the Middle East, Southeast Asia, and global financial centers such as London—and look at a best-practice player in each market.

The Middle East: Despite generally rigid Sharia boards and a high percentage of customers whose primary concern is product purity, competition is intensifying in this region as even the most conservative Muslims increasingly expect competitive pricing and returns (compared with conventional products), world-class service, and a wide-ranging product portfolio.

Indigenous, purely Islamic institutions may still have a superior level of local knowledge that can enhance customer acquisition and retention capabilities in the region. But multinationals are using their globally tested brand names and sales and distribution skills to capture share through their Islamic subsidiaries and windows.

One best-practice player in the region is Al Rajhi Bank, currently the largest Islamic bank in Saudi Arabia. Among its key success factors has been its relatively broad range of Islamic products compared with those of local competitors. The bank also has a somewhat diverse brand proposition in that it positions itself in Saudi Arabia as a pure-play Islamic bank for conservative Muslims, while in Malaysia, where it has ambitious expansion plans, it tries to appeal to a broad range of consumers on the basis of high standards of integrity and trust.

Southeast Asia: Sharia boards are somewhat more liberal in Southeast Asia, and Muslim clients there tend to be more open to conventional offerings. Just as in the Middle East, however, competition is heating up.

Kuala Lumpur has emerged as an Islamic financial center similar to Dubai and Bahrain, reflecting the importance of the Malaysian market. Many conventional Malaysian banks have launched Islamic capital-market offerings, leveraging their know-how in traditional products, and have tapped growing regional demand for

Sharia-compliant vehicles in retail and corporate banking, as well as in asset management. In addition, the Central Bank of Malaysia is encouraging growth through tax incentives, the issuing of new licenses (which has increased the presence of foreign players), and legislation allowing foreign ownership of up to 49 percent in local Islamic banks.

RHB Islamic Bank, the Islamic arm of Malaysia's fourth-largest banking group, has demonstrated many best practices, gaining initial success through its 2006 issue of a highly innovative sukuk to finance the Mukah power plant project. This was quickly followed by the launch of new products such as Equity Home Financing-i, which delivers features of a conventional mortgage package but is Sharia compliant. RHB Islamic Bank has also become the first financial institution in Malaysia to launch an innovative and fully Sharia-compliant IT system.

Global Financial Centers: Islamic banking is also growing in such global financial centers as London, Zurich, and Hong Kong. In the United Kingdom, investment-banking and asset-management products have thus far been the most prominent offerings. The UK retail market is still quite small, with great potential for growth.

London is, of course, a major hub for HSBC—a multinational player seeking to establish a footprint in Islamic banking around the world. The bank's Islamic division, HSBC Amanah, offers a wide range of retail products through its branches in Malaysia, the United Arab Emirates, Saudi Arabia, and the United Kingdom. It also offers corporate and investment-banking products globally, with a strong focus on sukuk issuance. Among HSBC Amanah's key success factors have been its large presence in the Middle East and its separate brand name, which signals that Islamic offerings are distinct from conventional products available under the broader HSBC umbrella. HSBC Amanah has also leveraged its conventional product-development expertise to structure comparable offerings that are Sharia compliant.

In other financial centers such as Zurich and Geneva, the current focus is on leveraging deep and long-term relationships with wealthy Muslim clients from the Middle East who are seeking Islamic private-banking services. In Asia, Hong Kong's position as a gateway to China is attracting Middle Eastern institutions wishing to invest petrodollars in China through Sharia-compliant vehicles.

Big Opportunity, Big Challenges

Why should banks with global and regional aspirations at least explore building a position in Islamic banking? There are some compelling reasons.

Finding new sources of growth is a challenge for virtually all banks. Given the large (and rapidly expanding) Muslim population worldwide and the relatively low level of Islamic banking penetration in many markets, the growth opportunity is undeniable. In addition to the markets discussed above, large Muslim populations exist in fast-growing, still-emerging economies such as Indonesia, Pakistan, Turkey, and North Africa. Islamic banking offerings can provide banks with an entry into such markets.

What is more, Islamic banking is not just for Muslims. Nor is it in any way arcane or esoteric. At its core, it is banking that follows a stringent set of principles, aims to be socially and ethically responsible, and embraces high transparency and shared risk. Successful marketing campaigns targeted at non-Muslims emphasize just such characteristics. Indeed, some pundits have drawn an analogy between Islamic banking products and various types of cuisine that are prepared under strict, faith-based guidelines—but are nonetheless appealing to the general population.

Obviously, however, just entering the Islamic banking market is a far cry from succeeding in it over the long-term. The challenges are substantial and numerous. They include the following:

Product Innovation. The fact that many banks, especially in the Middle East, are short on manufacturing capabilities to develop attractive Islamic products prevents them from absorbing inexpensive excess liquidity in the market. Long-term winners will be those banks that dedicate sufficient resources to structuring the most innovative Sharia-compliant products and that tailor those products to specific markets and segments.

Regulation. Divergent views on what is Sharia compliant, even within regions, hamper knowledge sharing and international cooperation. Also, a shortage of Sharia experts is forecast as the market grows. The first player to achieve a truly global Sharia board, thus enabling more efficient product development and distribution, will have a distinct competitive advantage.

Incorporation. In the Middle East, where Sharia councils are strictest, players may eventually need to move to a cooperative corporate structure in which there is no potential conflict with benefits distributed to customers being, in effect, subsidized by shareholders.

Risk. The Islamic banking industry needs common and internationally accepted standards on capital adequacy, risk, and asset-quality assessment. It also needs standardized financial reporting and disclosure rules across all markets. Achieving these goals would bring Islamic institutions up to the level of leading conventional banks, allow investors to better compare performance, and avoid further fragmentation in the industry. Furthermore, on an individual bank level, new Islamic products can potentially cannibalize traditional ones and, if not managed properly, lead to unwanted organizational complexity.

Talent. A war for talent is in progress among Islamic banks and between Islamic and conventional banks for individuals who have top-flight sales skills and understand Sharia principles. Players that develop the most aggressive and efficient internal training programs to counteract the scarcity of qualified personnel in the market will have an advantage.

Over the past few years, Islamic banking has been one of the fastest-growing banking segments globally. According to some estimates, global Islamic banking assets may reach $1 trillion within a few years. Our own research confirms that best-practice players have a surprisingly high number of non-Muslims in their customer bases. Overall, however, the industry is still in an early stage of development, and opportunity abounds.

If your financial institution is looking for new ways to grow, you should consider taking the following steps:

- Assess the appeal of Islamic banking products to your current customer base and to consumers in regions where you have growth aspirations. Gauge the extent to which your target markets are already penetrated.
- Survey your non-Muslim customers who have shown a penchant for socially conscious financial products. Determine their interest in Islamic banking. Research marketing approaches—both local and regional—to these customers and to your general customer base.

- Explore your in-house capacity to develop a Sharia council that could aid product development issues. Examine ways to access external expertise on Sharia compliance. Engage your innovation staff to formulate potential new Islamic products.
- Scan your branch network to identify cities and regions where Muslims make up a large percentage of the population. These locations could host a pilot project.
- Investigate whether an entry into Islamic banking might best be attempted through a potential acquisition, as opposed to organically.

Above all, major banks need to make a decision—sooner rather than later—regarding whether or not to pursue the Islamic banking opportunity. Institutions that decide to enter the arena will need to rapidly achieve clarity on their specific visions and aspirations.

Players that decide to stay out of the game may have good reasons for holding back. But if Islamic banking does become one of the next big things in financial services, the early movers will gain a valuable head start on mining a potentially deep source of long-term growth.

(Vincent Chin and Knut Storholm are partners and managing directors in the Singapore office of The Boston Consulting Group. Sven-Olaf Vathje is a partner and managing director in the firm's Frankfurt office. Nor Azah Razali is a principal in BCG's Kuala Lumpur office. Mohammed Badi is a project leader in the firm's New York office. They can be reached at chin.vincent@bcg.com, storholm.knut@bcg.com, vathje.sven-olaf@bcg.com, razali.nor.azah@bcg.com and badi.mohammed@bcg.com respectively.)

3

Islamic Financing Arrangements used in Islamic Banking

Ehsan Zarrokh

Islamic finance is an old concept but a very young discipline in the academic sense. It lacks the required extent and level of theories and models needed for expansion and implementation of the framework provided by Islam. In these circumstances, unawareness and confusion exist as to the form of the Islamic financial system and instruments.

The main difference between the present economic system and the Islamic economic system is that the latter is based on keeping in view certain social objectives for the benefit of human beings and society. Islam, through its various principles, guides human life and ensures free enterprise and trade. That is the reason why the conventional banker does not have to be concerned with the moral implications of the business venture for which money is lent.

Socio-economic justice is central to the Islamic way of life. Every religion has the same basic aim. In an Islamic environment, an individual not only lives for himself, but his scope of activities and responsibilities extend beyond him to the welfare and interests of society at large. The KORAN is very precise and clear on this issue. There are basically three components of an Islamic economic paradigm:

1. That as vice-regent, man should seek the bounties of the land that God has bestowed on humanity. From the wealth thus obtained, he should enjoy his own share.
2. That he should be magnanimous to others and use a part of the wealth so obtained also for the benefit of his fellow-beings.
3. That his actions should not be willfully damaging to his fellow-beings.

Human society in Islam is based upon the validity of law, of life and the validity of mankind. All these are natural corollaries of the faith. Islamic laws promote the welfare of people by safeguarding their faith, life, intellect, property and their posterity. God nurtures, nourishes, sustains, develops and leads humanity towards perfection. Even though an individual may be making a living because of his efforts, he is not the only one contributing towards that living. There are a number of divine inputs into this effort and therefore, the results of such an effort obviously cannot be construed as entirely proprietary.

Whereas the Islamic banker has a much greater responsibility. This leads us to a very fundamental concept of the Islamic financial system i.e., the relation of investors to the institution is that of partners whereas that of conventional banking is that of creditor-investor.

The Islamic financial system is based on equity whereas the conventional banking system is loan based. Islam is not against the earning of money. In fact, Islam prohibits earning of money through unfair trading practices and other activities that are socially harmful in one way or another. [1]

Those who swallow down usury cannot arise except as one whom Shaitan (evil) has prostrated by (his) touch does rise. That is because they say, trading is only like usury; and Allah has allowed trading and forbidden usury. To whomsoever then the admonition has come from his Lord, then he desists, he shall have what has already passed, and his affair is in the hands of Allah; and whoever returns (to it) – these are the inmates of the fire; they shall abide in it [Surah 2:275].

Not that there was any ambiguity in the Command of Allah. Far be it from Him to give any order to His Servants, which they can not comprehend. The fact is that those who had surplus money and wanted to earn profit did so either by lending it through RIBA (usury) or by investing it in trade and hypocrites were not prepared to forgo the first option. Hence, they argued that since both were means of earning profit, they were alike and the prohibition of RIBA did not stand to reason.

The practice of RIBA i.e., usury was so deep-rooted in society and continuance of the practice was so undesirable, that Allah warned the believers that if they did not desist, they should be prepared for a war against Allah and His Apostle. This warning was heeded by the Muslim Ummah and for more than a thousand years the economies of Muslim states were free from Riba. With the ascendancy of Western influence and its suzerainty over Muslim states, the position changed and an interest-based economy became acceptable. Efforts in Muslim countries to revert to an interest-free economy were hampered by many obstacles. [2]

The Role of Money

The traditional definition of the time value of money leads one to assume that profit maximization is the objective of investors irrespective of whether or not the earning of profit has made someone else worse off. Some economists have termed the maximization of profit as the sole objective of corporations. This view cannot be supported or defended since the profit maximization process may lead to perverse outcomes. When financial operations are removed of moralistic tone, competitive markets fail to achieve the efficient allocation of a country's resources.

In Islam money in itself is not considered, as actual capital only exists when money, along with other resources, is sunk into productive activities. Linking the use of money to productive purposes invariably brings into action the factor of labor, a process from which benefits pass on to society.

Types of Islamic Financial Instruments

Demand for monetary instruments is influenced by the variation and level in the market rate what is meant as the market rate of return. The demand for household monetary instruments is mainly for the purpose of circulation of income. Banks need these instruments for:

1. Transaction purposes;
2. Precautionary purposes, in that some unexpected payments have to be made while some expected inflows may not be forthcoming on their due date, and;
3. Not only to avoid loss but also to obtain gains in the capital value of financial assets under the expectation that the market rate of return may move in a certain direction.

What differentiates a traditional financial market from others markets is that no tangible good or service is exchanged for any monetary consideration; only a "financial claim" changes hands in the form of a promissory note or a title to any future flow of income adjusted for any capital appreciation. Not all Islamic instruments are purely financial claims. Some of the instruments also represent ownership of the underlying assets together with a claim to underlying cash flows. Basically there are the following four types of Islamic financial instruments:

Type "A" is a financial claim of monetary value with recourse to underlying durable assets and related cash flows. This type has a predictable future income stream, is marketable and can be discounted since with the changing of hands, the instrument passes title to the goods and not to the debt. It is basically lease-based.

Type "B" is instrument is partly backed by durable assets and its income is not predictable, but evaluated through an asset valuation process at the end of an agreed and declared duration. The underlying transactions can be a mix of IJARA, Modaraba, Musharaka etc., contracts. This Type may be traded in the secondary market at its fair market price acceptable to the parties involved but not discounted.

Type "C" is purely a monetary claim to an expected income stream forthcoming from underlying commercial transactions. Income is evaluated through an asset-valuation process at the end of an agreed and declared period. A transaction of this type may comprise Morabaha, Istasna etc., contracts which are debt claims against third parties in respect to actual commercial transactions. The Type may be traded at its face value declared at the end of each accounting period but cannot be discounted.

The Type "D" is purely a financial claim of monetary value but with recourse to certain precious metals such as gold, silver, platinum, etc., or commodities quoted on exchanges. The instrument entitles the holder to take delivery of the underlying asset but does not carry any attached revenue stream except that its price is pegged to the price of the underlying precious metal or commodity quoted at recognized international exchange rates. It can be traded but not discounted. [3]

Risk Mitigating Features

The phenomenon of risk plays a pervasive role in economic life. Without it, financial and capital markets would consist of the exchange of a single instrument each period, the communications industry would cease to exist in so far as this market is concerned and the profession of investment banking would be reduced to that of accounting. Risk is further segregated from uncertainty. A situation is said to involve risk if the randomness facing an economic agent can be expressed in terms of specific numerical probabilities (these probabilities may either be objectively specified, as with lottery tickets or else reflect the individual's own subjective beliefs). Situations where the agent cannot (or does not) assign actual probabilities to alternative possible occurrences are said to involve uncertainty.

While it is not always true that a riskier asset will pay a higher average rate of return, it is usually return. Risk is an opportunity in financial markets and also a problem. Risk-averse investors require additional return to be at additional risk and, in effect, in a competitive market higher return is accompanied by higher risk. An investor evaluates an asset in terms of its marginal contribution to his/her portfolio.

The fundamental principal of valuation is that the value of any financial asset is the present value of the cash expected. The process requires two steps:

1. Estimating the cash flow, and;
2. Determining the appropriate interest rate that should be used to calculate the present value.

The following are the Shari'ah compliant risk mitigating features:

1. By prior arrangements in the instrument, the investing company, through its banker, would have a priori right in profit sharing up to an agreed upon ratio.

2. The profit will be paid on account on a monthly basis to the investing company as provided in the projected accounts.
3. The final accounting and settlement is accomplished at the end of the term of the instrument when the profit and loss accounts are finalized.
4. In order to mitigate the risk and as per the terms of the instrument, a Takaful fund is established for the term of the instrument.
5. In this Takaful fund where the invested company earmarks a part of their reserves for the Takaful fund.
6. The investing company will contribute 1% of the invested amount.
7. This 1% contribution is made through an advance by the invested company on account of future profits.
8. In case of any loss during the tenancy of the instrument, it will be adjusted against the Takaful fund.
9. The balance will be distributed between investor and at the end of the term of instrument.
10. Through a valuation, value of the investment would be established for the purpose of exercising the put option.
11. The investing company shall have the option to exercise its put option at the value price and the company shall buy this instrument. [4]

Islamic Leasing

But before describing leasing, as aforesaid, let me very briefly touch upon two of the basic or fundamental principles of Islamic finance in order to develop a premise for meaningful discussions on leasing.

It has to be asset-based financing:

The first fundamental principle of Shari'ah is that as opposed to conventional monetary dealing, profit is generated when something having intrinsic utility is sold or offered for use. Money has no intrinsic value. As such dealing in money (same currency) cannot generate profit but a Riba unless converted into real assets to deal with.

There has to be an element of risk:

The second basic element of Shari'ah is that one cannot claim a profit or fee for a property/transaction, the risk of which was never borne by him.

Based on the above fundamental principles, the most ideal mode or instrument of financing in Shari'ah are Musharaka and Mudaraba followed by Salam and Istinsa.

Morabaha and leasing are not originally modes of finance. However, to meet certain specific needs where ideal modes like Musharaka or Mudaraba are not workable for whatever reasons, they have been reshaped and allowed in Shari'ah subject to certain conditions.

Leasing described for leasing, Ijarah is an Arabic term with origins in Islamic Fiqh, meaning to give something to rent. There are two types of Ijareh. One relates to employing or hiring the services of a person for wages whereas the second type relates to the hiring of any asset or property in order to reap its benefits without the transfer of ownership, or what is called in English "Usufrukt". The price or consideration of this is the rent.

It is the second type of Ijareh which is the subject matter of the discussion here because it is generally used as a form of investment and also as a means of finance.

As described earlier, in the light of the two basic cornerstones of Shari'ah leasing is a contract whereby usufruct rights to an asset are transferred by the owner, known as the lessor, to another person, known as the lessee, at an agreed-upon price called the rent, and for an agreed-upon period of time called the term of lease.

Lease as a mode of financing strictly speaking leasing is not a means of finance as originally envisaged. It is simply a transaction much as a sale/purchase. As described above, the leasing transaction simply denotes the transfer of the usufruct of a property from one person to another for an agreed-upon price called rent without transferring the corpus i.e. ownership of that asset. Accordingly, the rules of "leasing" closely resemble the rules governing "sale" because in both cases something is transferred to second person for valuable consideration.

Leasing differs from sale only in-so-much-as not transferring the corpus or ownership of the property which remains with the transferor. As such in Shari'ah, a lease transaction is governed by a separate set of rules, which we shall outline in the following paragraphs.

Although leasing, as originally conceived, is not a means of finance, the financial institutions and the corporate world have adopted it as such. Due to several factors (including tax concessions, etc.), instead of providing an interest-bearing loan, certain financial institutions in the West started to provide requisite equipment to their customers. To arrive at the rent, the total cost of the asset is calculated plus interest or mark-up to be recovered during the period of lease on a monthly or quarterly basis. This type of lease in the West is known as a finance lease, to be distinguished from an operating lease, wherein various basic features of the leasing transaction are ignored which is tantamount to Riba.

Knowing that leasing is lawfully allowed under Shari'ah, since it meets one of the basic criteria of asset-based finance, a number of Islamic financial institutions have adopted leasing on this model as carried out by conventional financial institutions without making the necessary modifications that really conform to the rules under Shari'ah, particularly in regards to assuming the risk of ownership in the leased asset. Great care needs to be exercised to ensure various Shari'ah requirements, as rendered below, based on the basic two principles of:

- Asset based finance, and;
- Assuming a risk element connected to the ownership of the asset .

Basic Rules of Leasing

The description or definition given above, under part A, contains the following essential ingredients for outlining the basic rules under Shari'ah:

- That it is a contractual obligation.
- That there has to be a valuable use of the asset and transferability of that usufruct.
- That the ownership of the asset is retained by the transferor or lessor throughout the lease period. Consumable articles cannot be leased.

- That the risk and liabilities of ownership lie with the lessor. The leased asset shall remain the risk of the lessor throughout the lease period. Any loss or harm caused by factors beyond the control of the lessee shall be borne by the lessor. However, the lessee is liable to compensate the lessor for any harm to the leased asset caused by any misuse or negligence on the part of the lessee.
- That the risk and liabilities associated with the use of the asset shall be borne by the lessee. For instance, taxes and other government levies, utilities, etc. However, the contract must specify these items for clarity's sake.
- That the term of the lease, period of the lease, its renewal or early termination must be stipulated.
- Purpose of use. The lessee cannot use the leased assets other than for the purpose specified in the contract or agreed to by the lessor expressly.
- Commencement of lease. The lease commences from the date of delivery of the asset to the lessee and not from the day of payment or lease agreement, with reference to the commencement of rentals.
- Determination of rental. The rent for the entire period of the lease must be determined at the time of the contract. Different rates of rent for different phases during the lease period are permissible. This point will be elaborated in the following discussion of the issues.

Issues

While operating a leasing business, a number of practical issues have cropped up which warrant discussion and interpretation under Sharia'h. An exhaustive and conclusive list of such issues is impossible to make. However, certain important and salient issues need to be taken up in these discussions as follows:

- Joint ownership (Lessors)/Joint Lessees – (permissible)
- Insurance – Islamic Takaful – (by the owner)
- Renewal of or variation in the lease period – (permissible if mutually agreed-upon)
- Future date. Agreement to commence lease on some future date is allowed. However, the rent has to commence from the date of delivery. If the lessee has

paid the price and delivery of the asset is delayed by the supplier, then no rent is liable to be paid for the period of delay. It must be noted that future or forward sale in sale/purchase transaction is not permissible in Shari'ah. This is another major point after ownership transfer which differentiates leasing from a sale/purchase transaction under Shari'ah.

- Acquisition of an asset by the lessee. For various reasons, the asset subject to lease may be acquired by the lessee and payment may be disbursed. Through him by the lessor. This is permissible under Shari'ah on the principles of agent and principal. Here there are two relationships separate from and independent of one and other. The first relationship is that before becoming a lessee, an individual acts as an agent for and behalf of the lessor to acquire the asset. This is an independent arrangement. Once the asset has been acquired with all the risk and reward of ownership to the lessor, then a second relationship is created i.e. the lessor and the lessee under the lease agreement. That cost of acquisition shall be borne by the lessor being owner and not by the lessee.

Rentals

- Advance rentals are admissible subject to the condition of adjustment against the actual rental when due upon commencement of the lease as discussed before.
- Unilateral increase by the lessor is not permissible even if stipulated in the contract.
- *Bench marks.* The fixing of any bench mark for determining the amount of rent, as with an inflation index etc., is permissible provided that the lease agreement clearly stipulates the same e.g., if the inflation rate as declared by an authoritative body like the State Bank etc. is said to be 10% per annum, then the rent can be increased every year by that percentage.
- *Penalty for late payment of rentals.* Penalty or compensation for late payment is not permissible. Rentals once due become a debt obligation or monetary asset which cannot generate profit under Shari'ah. This situation has been exploited by unscrupulous lessees. In such circumstances, contemporary scholars have provided a solution whereby a penalty can be charged to the lessee for delayed payment though the amount recovered is only to be used for charitable purposes

by the lessor. In other words, the late payment charges cannot be taken as income by the lessor. A suitable clause, therefore, is to be incorporated into the lease agreement to avoid any misunderstanding in this regard.

- *Premature termination of lease.* Premature termination of lease is allowed provided that the lessee has violated or contravened the terms of the lease or it is by mutual consent of the lessee and the lessor. Any unilateral or unconditional termination of the lease either by the lessor or the lessee without prior notification is contrary to the principles of justice and equity, hence not allowed under Shari'ah.
- *Repossession of an asset.* In the event of early termination, or upon maturity of the term of lease, assets have to return to the lessor unless he voluntarily relinquishes his rights or makes a gift of the leased assets to the lessee. However, rent would be payable only up to the date of termination and not beyond. Entitlement or the right of the lessor to claim rent from any period after termination, even if expressly stipulated in the contract, is not valid under Shari'ah.
- *Residual value.* It is accepted under Shari'ah that ownership of the asset belongs to the lessor and, therefore, assets should revert back to him upon expiry of the lease. Any stipulation to the contrary in the contract that the lessor can sell or transfer the asset to the lessee upon the expiry of the term of the lease at a pre-determined price called residual value is not considered valid from the point of view of Shari'ah However, this point is currently a subject matter of debate among contemporary scholars. They are of the view that if a lessor unilaterally undertakes or promises to transfer the ownership to the lessee as a gift or at a token price separate from the lease agreement, then this can be considered validly binding on the lessor at the option of the lessee.
- What is important is that under Shari'ah the leasing and sale/purchase transactions are two separate things and should not be mixed up in one contract, as both are independent and governed by separate rules. Nothing, however, in Shari'ah stops the lessor from giving away the ownership of his assets at his own discretion or good will toward the lessee at any mutually agreed-upon price or as a gift upon the expiry of the leasing contract.

- *Sale and lease back.* This is allowed, but only as two separate transactions. That in the first place there is a sale of assets to be purchased by the lessor. This is governed by Shari'ah rules of sale/purchase at a fair market value. Once the ownership title is validly passed on to the lessee, a lease transaction can then be executed separately through a lease agreement.
- *Sub-lease.* Sub-lease by the lessee is permissible under Shari'ah subject to the consent of the lessor and can be expressly outlined in the lease agreement. In Shari'ah, however, there are divergent views if the rent arising from the sub-lease is higher than the rent payable on the original lease. Some scholars allow the differential to be retained by the lessee while others feel that the surplus received from the sub-lease should be passed on to the owner i.e. main lessor.
- *Assigning of the lease.* Also permissible under Shari'ah, the lessor can sell the leased assets to a third party along with his rights and obligations. The relationship between lessor and lessee in this case will be determined between the new owner and the lessee. However, the lessor cannot assign the lease without transferring the ownership for monetary consideration. Here the basic Shari'ah cornerstone of asset-back transaction is not there. Rent receivables are debt obligation which cannot, therefore, be transacted for a monetary price. Assignment of lease rentals without monetary consideration is, however, not prohibited in Shari'ah.
- *Securing of the lease.* Leased assets can be secured along the same principles governing the assignment i.e., ownership of assets along with the rent. Rent alone without ownership of the assets cannot be secured for the reason of being a debt obligation as discussed before. Securing a lease can be made wholly or partly to one party or to a number of persons. Documentation has to be carefully prepared to ensure the securing instrument represents assets and not the debt or monetary obligation alone. [5]

Some Difficulties

Major hurdles faced by Islamic finance houses are the absence of a necessary legal framework and the lack of adequate infrastructure in the banking and investment fields. [6]

The modern banking system is based on the concept that money should be treated like any other factor of production and must earn some return over a period of time. It is argued that the establishment of large-scale enterprises, and hence material progress, is not possible unless there is an agency that can mobilize financial resources from the public by paying them some interest, while lending these resources to entrepreneurs. By charging these entrepreneurs a higher interest, these agencies were able to utilize the difference (called a spread) to meet their expenses and to make some profit for the owners of the agency (i.e. share-holders). Banks were established to fulfill this need and from the beginning were only authorized to perform this function. They were legally prohibited from entering into trade or industry. When the Government of Iran decided to introduce an interest-free banking system, this prohibition was removed. After a lot of in-house the banks were told that they were allowed to deal in only 1 to 12 means of financing (only two were classified as "Financing by Lending").

These two permitted lending without interest by charging the actual expense incurred by the banks to meet their cost of operation and Qarde Al'hasana. All the rest were either trade-related or investment-type models. These included the purchase of goods by banks and their sale to clients at an appropriate mark-up price on a deferred payment basis, in case of default there being no further mark-up. This sale of goods on mark-up is known as Murabiha. Other types of financing were hire-purchase, leasing, Musharaka or profit-and-loss-sharing, equity participation and purchase of shares, etc.

Since Murabiha was the type nearest to lending and since it did not require any expertise in buying and selling commodities, bankers limited most of their financing to this type. In order to eliminate the risk of prospective buyers refusing to accept goods purchased by the banks by reason of not being strictly in accordance with the specifications, banks were allowed to appoint the prospective buyer as their agent for the purchase of the goods and later for the sale of the goods to the buyer's firm. Furthermore, to give as much leeway to the banks, as safeguards of public money, as possible, the Ulama did not fix a waiting period between the two stages of buying and selling.

The banks did not assume the role of trader and Morabiha degenerated into lending on mark-up. The banks rarely hired persons who knew even the basics of trading, nor did they train their existing staff to learn the art. They did not even bother to find out whether their agents had actually purchased the goods or not. The inability or reluctance of banks and financial institutions to change over their operations from lending to trading has been a serious impediment to the Islamisation of the economy.

The blame does not entirely fall on the bankers. Depositors have become so accustomed to their money remaining safe and yet earning profit that if a bank had really ventured to trade and incurred a slight loss, then the depositors would have immediately demanded their money back causing the bank to go bankrupt. In the existing state of morality this was more likely to happen. It actually did happen to a few investment companies that had started with good intention, but could not go on giving away handsome profits to their depositors.

A lack of seriousness and dedication in those responsible for the implementation was also another great impediment to the achievement the goal of an interest-free economy. Many of these individuals thought that in the present world, there was no alternative to interest, yet something had to be done because of demands from the government. Some, who were more influenced by Western education and culture, thought that interest banking was not prohibited by Islam. Yet others thought that the efforts being made were only superficial and in reality the new system was no different from the existing system.

One weakness in the implementation of the proposals to eliminate interest from the system was that people were not sufficiently motivated to sacrifice a part of their financial interests for the sake of carrying out the commands of Allah (SWT), and the Prophet (SAW). Anyone attempting to change a well-established practice must be prepared to make some sacrifice for this, as arguably no noble cause has been achieved without any sacrifice. The prevailing level of public morality within the existing legal and taxation system of the state made it an up-hill struggle to rid the banking system of interest. And it remains so. Beyond this, there are many avenues of making profit that would have to be forgone and many types of modern banking services which also could not be provided by a bank working strictly on Islamic principles. For example, they could not keep their surplus cash in fixed or saving deposits. In spite of these difficulties, those who were engaged in the task of Islamisation took it upon themselves to portray as successful the reforms, while those who pointed out the difficulties were labeled as either a cynic or an opponent of the new system. Anyone who uttered a word of caution was regarded as someone who did not want the experiment of Islamisation to succeed. As a matter of fact, reward in the Hereafter (Aakhirat) should have been the main purpose of Islamisation. It might not have attracted many people, but the foundation would have been firm.

One great obstacle in the realisation of the goal of an interest-free economy has been absence of a proper environment. Unfortunately nothing has been done to produce an ideal or a near ideal Islamic environment by government or public leaders. The most important pre-requisite for the enforcement of Shari'ah is A'DL [translation!!!!!!]. Establishment of the rule of law and ensuring justice to aggrieved persons should be the first task of an Islamic state, yet nothing have been done to achieve this end.

One very important requirement of an ideal environment is an inflation-free economy. Inflation erodes the real value of money, meaning that when a person gives a sum of money on loan and receives the same amount back after one year, he has made a net loss. A major source of inflation is deficit financing. The printing of notes to meet budgetary deficit is in fact an injustice to the public, since the real value of their money is consequently eroded. In this respect too, the government's performance is very discouraging. Government borrowings at high interest rates and the quantum of the government's domestic and foreign debts has reached a level which cannot be sustained. There has also been no effort to change the taxation structure so as to bring it to conform to Shari'ah. [7]

Musharaka

Musharaka represents the most desirable form of Islamic financing arrangements. Yet, in terms of its ability to be an effective and efficient instrument for replacing interest-based transactions, it poses formidable problems.

The salient features of the Musharaka agreement, as practised by the commercial banks, were as follows:

- It was a short-term financing arrangement specific only to the parties to the contract.

- Investment by the banks was made in the form of the sanctioning of a funding limit to the client and the degree of employment of funds was determined on the basis of daily product of outstanding balances due to the bank.
- All participative funds, including equity, reserves and other non-debt capital was included in the definition of capital qualifying for profits.
- Profit sharing ratio was determined through negotiations within the boundaries specified by the SBP.
- Profits for the purpose of sharing were to be determined after apportioning a share of net-income as a management fee to the firm.
- Provisional profits, based on projected profits, were to be paid to the bank on quarterly basis, subject to a final adjustment on the basis of actual profits or losses.
- Shortfalls or excess profits were to be settled through the creation of a [participation] reserve fund, which would attempt to smooth out the payments to the bank.
- Losses, if any, were to be shared in strict proportion to the bank's investment in the total capital of the firm.
- Against the apportioned loss of the bank, ordinary shares were to be issued, which qualified for recon version in Musharaka investment under the original terms of the agreement in case profits accrued in future.
- Standard securities in the form of pledging and hypothecation stocks or the mortgaging of properties were required against Musharaka financing.

Some of these features of the instrument attracted criticism. For example, the profit sharing arrangement did not strictly conform to the requirements of Shari'ah particularly in the treatment of losses and the payment of provisional profits or their adjustment through the participation reserve. Secondly, despite being a sharing arrangement, the actual agreement was cast within the framework of a creditor-debtor relationship, and was also protected as such in law. Three, Musharaka also demanded securities which were akin to the relationship between a creditor and debtor. Finally, in the absence of a legal framework regulating the operation of Musharaka, there was no standardization of the agreement, and the terms and conditions of various agreements varied considerably.

Modaraba

Modaraba represents another of the more desirable forms of Islamic financing arrangements.

The salient features of Modaraba companies and their operations are as follows:

- Only registered companies or those established under specific laws are eligible to register as Modaraba companies.
- Modaraba can either be specific purpose or multi-purpose and can either be for a fixed term or in perpetuity.
- On fulfillment of certain conditions, and with the prior approval of the Registrar, Modaraba companies may float Modaraba on the stock exchange, and their certificates of issue will be tradable securities.
- Each Modaraba will be a separate business and its operations must conform to those approved under the injunctions of Shari'ah.
- A Religious Board, to be periodically constituted under the ordinance, will be empowered to declare whether the operations of Modaraba were in conformity with the provisions of Shari'ah or not.
- Many disclosure requirements, similar to those applicable to listed companies, are applicable to Modarabas, including statutory audit, annual meetings and investments and loans to and from the directors of the Modaraba Company.

Evidently, the entire scheme was an elegant formulation of the simple relationship required under a Modaraba contract between labor (Darib) and capital (Rabbulma'l). The management company was to be remunerated through a fixed management fee paid out of the net income of the Modaraba and the remainder was to go to Modaraba certificate holders, with adequate provisions for retained earnings to ensure future growth.

Conclusions

To outline the broad features of a strategy which holds the promise of successfully implementing an Islamic system of finance are as follows:

- The process has to be guided by basic legislative efforts covering all the essential elements of the proposed programme.
- The legislation would define Riba and prohibit transactions connected with Riba.
- The application of the law would be unqualified and without exception, thus the entire financial sector, covering banking government finance and foreign transactions would be covered in its ambit.
- Given the unqualified and non-exceptional nature of the proposed law, even existing relations will have to be converted into permissible forms, for which a suitable time frame, within a phasing-in period, will be allowed.
- The law should also provide for the Constitution of a Shari'ah Board which would assist the SBP to formulate permissible means of financing. Such means, specified with the prior approval of the Board, will only be illustrative and no restrictions will be placed on banks and financial institutions to design means of financing which are free of Riba.
- A major portion of the law will have to be devoted to a plan of restructuring the fiscal policy which comprises a scheme for the privatization of public sector assets and the use of its proceeds for the settlement of the outstanding stock of public debt.

The proposed strategy is based on the clear recognition of the scope implied by the prohibition of Riba. This is critical, for otherwise the solution will continue to elude us.

(Ehsan Zarrokh can be reached at Zarrokh2007@Yahoo.com)

4

Islamic Banking and Finance

Shari 'a-Compliance and the Reinterpretation of Riba

Sapana Shah

The growth of Islamic banking is symptomatic of the global demand of Shari 'a-compliant products. This growth illustrates not only the desire to follow the religious mandates and the spirit of Islam, but the social economic capabilities of such a popular system. The current tools are inadequate to fulfill such desires and expectations and provide some difficulty in becoming compatible with the Western banking system. The only solution would be to provide a moderate form of interest. As a matter of Islamic law, this could only be achieved by a second consensus to change the prevailing interpretation of riba. While some countries do endorse alternative views, as opposed to the classical view, a second consensus will render a uniform agreement of the boundaries of riba and provide a powerful movement towards a more equitable distribution of wealth.

I. Introduction

The Islamic financial framework is governed by *Shari 'a*, a "body of rules deriving its legitimacy from the theological premise that it is God's law."[1] Despite the controversial nature of state intervention and enforcement of Shari 'a principles, Islamic banking practices nonetheless purport to follow the precepts mandated under Shari 'a, particularly the Qur'an and the Sunna, the primary and secondary sources of Shari 'a. In recent years, Islamic banking practices and Shari 'a-compliant systems have significantly expanded throughout the world. Since its inception three decades ago, the number of Islamic financial institutions worldwide has risen from one in 1975 to over 300 today in more than 75 countries[2]. They are concentrated in the Middle East and Southeast Asia (with Bahrain and Malaysia the biggest hubs), but are also appearing in Europe and the United States[3]. Total assets worldwide are estimated to exceed $250 billion, and are growing at an estimated 15 percent a year[4].

Due to this expansion, most research of the Islamic banking movement concerns the compatibility of Islamic and Western banking structures. While I do compare and contrast these two structures, my analysis focuses more on the nature of the Shari 'a-compliant structures themselves. Specifically, I examine the underlying principles and whether the goals are being fulfilled. Qur'anic injunctions and Islamic narratives expressly disapprove of *riba*, or interest. Proponents have strictly interpreted this prohibition and created a financial system that is interest-free and predominantly risk sharing. However, what truly constitutes a prohibited increase? Thus, my thesis turns on this critical issue and I argue that riba should *not* be interpreted as the complete interdiction of interest.

My analysis will reveal that the prevailing interpretation of riba in the Islamic sources of law creates a deadlock for the implementation and creation of Shari 'a-compliant practices. I illustrate that 1) the concept of 'interest' is still prevalent in these models and is, therefore, hypocritical; and 2) the models only serve the interest of the wealthy, thereby acting counter-productively to the social justice imperatives of Islamic law. In turn, I assert that the only effective solution is to reinterpret riba for a moderate use of interest. A broader construction of riba would permit greater Shari 'a compliance and more equitable distribution of wealth.

II. Background

A. Definitions and Sources of Islamic Law

Shari 'a is the Arabic word for Islamic law and is also known as the 'Law of Allah.' It is important to note that Shari 'a governs all aspects of life and therefore does not distinguish between secular and religious life. There are two primary sources of law in Islam: the Qur'an and the Sunna. The Qur'an is the holy book of Islam and is considered to be the direct words of God and as spoken to the Prophet Muhammad[5]. The Sunna is the rule that is deduced from the sayings of the Prophet in his actions of pronouncement or his approval thereof, which was recorded or became part of tradition. The two last sources, Ijma and Qiyas, become necessary when the Qur'an and the Sunna are insufficient to address an issue. Ijma signifies 'consensus.' That is to say, something is found to be truthful or a rule because it was determined unanimously. Finally, Qiyas is the use of analogy, of something known to be true, to address an unknown situation. Under Shari 'a, these four sources constitute a hierarchy of importance, where the Qur'an is most significant and Qiyas is least. These sources serve as the foundation of Shari 'a and the basis for understanding Islamic banking law. It is evident that scope of Shari 'a is greater than what we ordinarily consider "law." Shari' a encompasses every segment of public and private life.

B. Objectives of Islamic Law

Understanding the goals of Islamic law generally is important to understand the meaning and reason behind specific Islamic banking regulations. According to Muslim legal theory, the "purpose of Islamic law is to seek after the righteous path – to try to come as close as possible to it, and in doing so achieve the welfare of the people."[6] This precept comes from the concept of oneness of God, or *Tawhid*[7]. Next is the notion that from this supreme being came humans, who are God's vicegerents, or *Khalifah* on earth[8]. As *Khalifah*, all human beings are considered equal and are to act in the best well-being of one another.

Thus, this purpose is *tahqiq masalih al-'ibad*: the idea that the pursuit of abstract values, such as justice, compassion and mercy, is supposed to translate into concrete and tangible benefits to be enjoyed by human beings[9]. Specifically, the concept of justice, or *adalah* is a central tenet of the Islamic faith and is a value that governs all aspects of Shari 'a.

The Qur'anic ideals of fairness and justice apply to financial affairs. One application of these Qur'anic principles to the area of economics is the following: "The methodology of how man uses resources and means of production to satisfy all his worldly needs, according to a predetermined God-given code in order to achieve the greatest equity."[10] There are five unique characteristics of how financial affairs are addressed in the Islamic faith:

1. Man, being an agent and not an original owner, is not a free agent in his exploitation of resources and must use methods and means within a framework given to him in the satisfaction of his economic means.
2. The guiding principle of economic activity is the overall good of society and nature (environmental).
3. Individual man, being part of the overall fabric, must be given consideration for his well being.
4. Equitable reward must be given to man according to his effort (to all according to their efforts, and from all according to their abilities).
5. Certain activities in the exploitation of resources, having over-all detrimental effects, are proscribed[11].

Essentially, Islamic law permits the accumulation of wealth and property ownership, however, only through socially conscious means and in consideration of the well-being of others.

III. Islamic Banking and Finance

The ideology of Islamic banking and finance was born in the 1970's based on the writings of Muhammad Iqbal and Abu Al-A'la Al- Maududi, Bakir Al- Sadr, and Sayidd Qutub[12]. Scholars urge that Islamic finance developed into a sub-field of economics for socio-political reasons. Developed alongside Western economics, the Islamic system of banking and finance was initially based on the Western, capitalist interest-based banking model. With the great influx of wealth and capital that resulted from the oil industry, Islamic banking structures felt an immediate need to rely on Western principles of capitalist banking. The spread of this form of banking system raised increasing realization that such a banking model was strictly prohibited under Islamic precepts and Shari 'a. This awareness fostered a strong resurgence to revive

Islamic ideals and galvanized the impetus to institute Shari 'a compliant banking practices. Perhaps the foremost necessity was to eradicate practices based on interest. Hence the Islamic world found itself in the need of an alternative banking model that was Shari 'a compliant and interest-free, and that also accomplished the same goals as the Western model: a system that would provide the same incentives to lenders and borrowers to enter into financial transactions. The challenge that faces the Islamic banking world today is finding the appropriate model to accomplish this goal. The proper form of an alternative banking models is a highly contested question. As a result, several modes have been proposed and I will discuss each of these finance structures in turn.

A. Principles of Islamic Banking

In order to be Shari 'a compliant, Islamic banking and finance must comport with the fundamental principles of Islamic law. With respect to Islamic banking and finance, this means that such as the notion that wealth accumulation must provide for the greater good of society. Banking practices need not be interest-free to satisfy this condition; rather, since Shari 'a prohibits the accumulation of wealth that is not the product of work, what is also specifically prohibited is capital in return for something that does not constitute work. In a similar vein, risk must lay with all parties in the transaction. Therefore, a model employing a fixed rate of return would violate Islamic principles; instead, Islamic financial transactions mandate the principle of shared risk allocation. Therefore, in order for the parties in a financial transaction to receive any benefit in addition to the principal amount invested, they must share the risks involved in the transaction. In bank transactions, the Islamic bank should share the risk with the consumer.

B. Prohibition of Riba and Gharar

1. Prohibition of Riba

The notion that Shari 'a permits the accumulation of wealth through socially conscious means indicates that there are a number of ways in which accumulation of wealth is prohibited or is *haram*. These forms include hoarding, gambling and betting in all forms; cheating in quality, quantity, weight or any specifications of the goods and services traded or acquired or disposed of; all types of fraudulent sale or sales used as an excuse to charge interest, trade malpractices (for example, creating artificial scarcities); and interest in any form and at any rate[13].

According to Islamic jurists, the prohibition of interest, or *riba*, is aimed at avoiding "the illegality of all forms of gain or profit which were unearned in the sense that they resulted from speculative or risky transactions and could not be precisely calculated in advance by the contracting parties."[14] Thus, riba signifies an unjustified increase that constitutes unjust enrichment because it fosters the accumulation of wealth that is not from the product of work.

On the community level, prohibiting riba ensures that wealth is accumulated for the benefit of the community[15]. This is demonstrated in the *zakat*, a compulsory wealth tax in the Qur'an, which must be paid to the poor annually[16]. The tax deters wealth from accumulating and concentrating in the hands of a small number of wealthy individuals. By limiting hoarding, the Qur'an encourages a "just return to all members of a society from socioeconomic development." Islamic scholars also posit that social justice is served because prohibiting riba discourages unequal bargaining by forcing investors to bear direct risks[17].

Scholars have also put forth purely economic reasons for the prohibition of riba. One argument is that because trade is a pre-determined cost of production, it tends to prevent full employment. Scholars have argued that the unjust allocation of risk between borrower and lender creates a "penalty upon entrepreneurial initiative."[18] In a truly competitive market, Islamic scholars believe it to be unlikely that an investment could result in gross profits that also cover the interest. Since capital would be unproductive without entrepreneurial input, the disincentive to create wealth hinders economic growth[19]. Similar arguments attributing the international monetary crises have also been made. Studies have not been successful in supporting these theories. Nonetheless, the predominant existing belief is that interest is harmful and exploitative, which is the reason it is prohibited in Islamic sources.

This prohibition of riba is evident in multiple sources of Islamic law: the Qur'an, Islamic records of history, and the Arabic language. The prohibition of riba is mentioned in four different revelations in the Qur'an. The first revelation states that interest deprives wealth of God's blessings[20]. The second revelation condemns interest, by comparing interest to the wrongful taking of property of others[21]. The third revelation opines that

Muslims should stay away from interest for their own sake and the sake of others.[22] The fourth revelation discusses the distinction between interest in trade. The premise of the dichotomy in the last revelation is that Muslims should take the principal sum, and to take this amount as long as the borrower is able to repay. The Qur'an indicates that those who disregard the prohibition of interest are at war with God and His Prophet. Specifically, the Qur'anic prohibition of riba reads:

> Those who devour [riba]
> Will not stand except
> As stands one whom
> The Evil One by his touch
> Hath driven to madness
> That is because they say:
> "[Sale] is like usury [(riba)]."
> But Allah hath permitted [sale]
> And forbidden [riba].
> Allah will deprive
> [Riba] of all blessing,
> But will give increase
> For [voluntary] deeds of charity;
> For He loveth not
> Creatures ungrateful And wicked[23].
> The Qur'an goes on to warn:
> That they took [riba],
> Though they were forbidden;
> And that they devoured
> Men's substance wrongfully -

We have prepared for those

Among them who reject Faith

A grievous punishment[24].

The prohibition of riba is also explicitly stated in the Sunna. For instance, one narrative from the authority, Abu Hurayrah relays,

"The Prophet, peace be upon him, said: 'On the night of Ascension I came upon people whose stomachs were like houses with snakes visible from the outside. I asked Gabriel who they were. He replied that they were people who had received riba.' (Musnad Ahmed)." [25]

Although the Sunna discusses riba in narrative form, the account clearly expresses the disapproval of riba. The Prophet condemned not only those who take interest but also those who give interest and those who record or witness the transaction, saying that they are all alike in guilt[26].

It may be mentioned in passing that similar prohibitions are to be found in the pre-Qur'anic scriptures, although the 'People of the Book', as the Qur'an refers to them, had chosen to rationalize them. It is amazing that Islam has successfully warded off various subsequent rationalization attempts aimed at legitimizing the institution of interest[27].

2. Interpreting Riba

There are varying interpretations of the Qur'an, and while there is a clear proscription of riba, the exact meaning of riba remains unclear. Some scholars maintain that there is a distinction between "riba" and "usury," whereby usury is the illegal and unjust collection of interest. The following Qur'anic verse illustrates this interpretation:

O ye who believe! Devour not Usury [riba], Doubled and multiplied;

But fear Allah; that Ye may (really) prosper[28].

As a pre-Islamic practice, the majority of those who lived at subsistence level, whose crops would be destroyed during famine or hostile raid, would seek money from lenders. If they could not repay this amount by the specified date, the sum of the amount would be increased, whereby the lender's profit would double and the borrower receives an extension at an exorbitant price[29]. The Hanbali school of Islamic law, declared that the practice of "pay or increase" is the only form of riba targeted by the Qur'an's prohibition that is beyond any doubt. All other occasions and aspects of "increase" in financial transactions remain subject to doubt, and therefore to disagreement, within the Islamic legal community as to whether the riba prohibition applies[30].

Most Islamic scholars, however, hold a strict interpretation of the Qur'an, or a Classical view, and opine that all forms of interest are prohibited under Shari 'a. Scholars hold that due to principles of social fairness and abuses delineated in historical sources, that all forms of interest riba constitute prohibited riba. They argue that the conventional banking system, based on interest, is fundamentally unjust: First, the management and owners of a bank are sophisticated and will use their market knowledge to increase profits and the institution's net worth[31]. Second, they are protected from their mistakes (arising from their willingness to take risks) by the state and the insurance companies whose premiums are in fact paid by lowering returns to depositors[32]. Third, since depositors are guaranteed a certain rate of return on their deposits, banks place the full risk of lending on the borrower[33]. The proponents of the Islamic banking movement have endorsed this strict interpretationist view and created financing tools that are purported to be "interest- free."

3. Prohibition of Gharar

A key counterpart to the prohibition of riba is the prohibition of *gharar*, a term which has been translated as "trading in risk," or "risk-taking." This has been understood as the ignorance of the material attributes of a transaction, such as existence of the subject matter, deliverability, terms, and timing of payment. The issue of gharar is traditionally overcome when the parties to a contract have adequate knowledge of the subject matter of the transaction and the counter-values they intend to exchange[34].

Just as riba, the exact definition of gharar is unknown and jurists disagree as to the extent of the prohibition of gharar. Jurists have debated the presence of gharar in those sales in which the object is not viewed before conclusion of the contract or in which the object is nonexistent at the time of entry into the contract[35]. While many have held that the gharar in these contracts are excessive, others have held it is minimal. If the prohibition of the sale for inexistent items deems the contract invalid, business concerning speculative trading, arbitrage and the like would be strongly impacted[36].

IV. State Implementation of Shari 'a-Compliant Structures

As far as state implementation of Shari 'a, countries vary in their codification of riba and use of Shari 'a-compliant tools. As mentioned in Part IV of this paper, most modern jurists hold a strict interpretation or a Classical view of riba, that all forms of interest are interdicted. Countries such as Sudan, Iran and Pakistan endorse this view; Sudan, specifically has made the charging of interest a criminal offense, punishable by lashing[37].

Other nations hold modern interpretations of riba and have codified it as such in their respective Constitutions. The Hanbali school's moderate use of riba is one modern approach. The Kuwaiti Civil and Commercial Codes are symptomatic of the discretionary application of riba. Here, the riba is forbidden in civil transactions, but *is* permitted in commercial transactions subject to a state-declared ceiling of 7%. Subsection (2) of Article 102 of the Kuwaiti Civil and Commercial Codes provides that where interest has been agreed upon and the debtor fails to pay, the deferred interest shall be calculated on the basis of the agreed-upon rate. Compound interest is prohibited and the sum of interest due should never exceed the sum of the loan capital, notwithstanding rates for long-term loans[38]. Countries such as Oman, Qatar and Bahrain accept such modern solutions[39].

V. Comparison to Western Institutions and Capitalist Systems

Current Islamic financing tools purport to provide interest-free options. As the demand for such options are growing, understanding the compatibility between the Shari 'a – compliant financial models and the conventional banking models has become increasingly central. While the global expansion of Shari 'a – compliant structures may imply that cooperation has been successful, the two types of structures inherently differ in their ideologies. I argue that whether or not riba is implemented, Islamic and Western banking methods fundamentally differ. This is not to say that they are not compatible, but rather that the incentives for profit are for different purposes and goals.

A. Sources of Law

The strongest distinction between Islamic jurisprudence and the Western counterpart, which directly correlates to the differences in banking and finance practices, are the distinct sources of law. In Islam, Shari 'a derives from both religious texts and history – the sources of analogy and reason are employed when the primary sources, the Qur'an and the Sunna are silent. Analogy and reason are then employed to create legal solutions and rules that are in the same vein as the Qur'an and the Sunna. In the Western world, law is derived from the human process—from legal scholars, judges, jurists and the like. This law evolves over time, as it interacts within societies and changes based on the circumstances of particular individuals.

The dichotomy between religious sources and the human process directly impacts the respective economic policies. Since Islamic law is based on religious precepts, its economic policies are also necessarily constructed based on religious aspects. In the Western regime, on the other hand, there is a separation of Church and State, which as a by- product, prevents economic policies to be based on religion.

B. Differences in Objectives and Principles of Interest

The varying ideologies between Islamic law and Western law, embedded in their legal sources, engenders many points of divergence between Islamic and the Western economic policies.

The Western view of interest is one primary form of distinction. In a capitalist system, making a profit off of an investment, usually in the form of interest, is the key incentive to invest. For instance, for an investor, the incentive to invest in a fund is that the principal amount of money will over time yield a value equal to a certain percentage rate. Similarly, a bank loans money on the basis that it will receive a profit from adding a percentage to the amount to be repaid. With such differing view of "interest," clearly consolidating Islamic and Western banking models necessitate a compatibility of two ideological ends.

VI. Shari 'a Compliant Model v. the Western Model

There are significant practical distinctions between a Shari'a—compliant model and the Western model. The issue of risk is one of the most distinguishing features of the banking systems. In traditional banking, the owners of the bank are more at risk than the depositors. The only time when the depositors' funds are at risk is when the losses are so large that even the capital is written off. Likewise, if there is a banking failure under conventional banking, depositors are guaranteed up to $100,000 per account[40].

In Islamic banking, on the other hand, "Islamic bank will mediate the relationship between its aggregate depositors and its aggregate borrowers."[41] If the Islamic bank is profitable, the depositors are entitled to a share of those profits. If there are losses, then these as well are distributed to the depositors. The central argument, therefore, is that the owners of the bank are not necessarily more at risk than the depositors, nor are depositors afforded such strong protection as in conventional banking.

Another important area is pricing. For traditional banks, banks will charge the highest interest rate in which they could make a profit, which is low enough to maintain customers and remain competitive. This pricing, that is dependent on the market, will cover certain required expenses for the traditional bank: the expenses for running a bank, a reservation for bad loans, regulatory procedures, and the cost of funds of the bank. The cost of funds for the traditional bank is equivalent to the interest payments.

Islamic banks on the other hand, as mentioned earlier, are based on a profit-sharing transaction. Thus, the bank will attempt to obtain a minimum return on the loan. The minimum return will be computed the same as the traditional bank, with the exception of the cost of funds. As such, the Islamic bank has the same costs; however, instead of interest payments for the costs of funds, the Islamic bank pays their depositors an amount corresponding to the expected profit or loss from investment and lending activities[42].

VII. Forms of Shari 'a-Compliant Banking Practices

Several Islamic financial models have been proposed in an attempt to comply with Islamic precepts while at the same time providing the incentives of capitalist banking systems. As stated earlier, there has been no clear consensus for an efficient model. Rather, several approaches accomplish these goals and fall into the following categories: (1) non-fund transactions, (2) investment activities, and (3) social activities[43]. Non-fund transactions refer to conventional banking practices, which are service-oriented transactions between banks and depositors. Such transactions include depositing and withdrawing money from banks, all of which is interest-free. Investment activities refer to practices involved with capital financing for industries and trade. The common investment activity tools are the following: *mudaraba, musharaka, murabaha, bai'muajjal, ijara,* and *bai'salam.*

A. Mudaraba

Mudaraba is a profit-and-loss sharing financial system, which is equivalent to venture capitalism. In this type of transaction, an investor trusts an entrepreneur with capital; if the entrepreneur makes a profit, then he would agree to share a certain percentage with the investor yet would be free of any losses. Hence, if there are any losses of capital, only the investor bears the financial loss. Mudaraba is one of the most basic forms of Islamic banking.

This arrangement avoids the use of riba. Some may argue that because the entrepreneur does not share the financial loss, that the risk only falls upon the investor, thereby violating the Islamic mandate of risk- sharing. Many Islamic jurists counter this proposition by asserting that the entrepreneur does assume the risk and potential loss of time and effort. It appears that this latter view is heavily supported, perhaps in light of the fact that the Prophet has approved the practice of mudaraba.

B. Musharaka

Musharaka is a capitalistic partnership agreement, whereby investors contribute capital together, sharing the losses and profits on an agreed-upon equation. In this arrangement, clearly without the use of riba, the losses and profits are shared among the participants. Like mudaraba, musharaka is also one of the most basic forms of Islamic banking.

C. Murabaha

Murabaha constitutes financing on a "cost plus" basis. Here, the bank purchases goods at a certain price and resells it to customers at a higher price. Under traditional banking, the customer would likely incur fees or interest calculations if there is a default. Under murabaha, the customer is only liable for the contracted good.

One salient argument is that the discrepancy in price may serve as riba to the customer. The signal response is that the nature of the transaction places a risk on the bank as well. In other words, earning a profit by reselling the goods at a higher price is justified because the bank carries the risk of customers refusing to accept the goods. This form of banking is considered practically less risky than mudaraba and musharaka, and therefore is a more common practice.

The following is a typical business transaction that could be used under a murabaha financial tool. Suppose a businessman wishes to go into business selling sailboats. If the businessman's credit history is approved, then a conventional bank would grant a cash loan. At this point, the businessman would use the proceeds to buy the sailboats, and meanwhile owe the bank the funds while paying interest along the way. However, under a murabaha transaction, the bank would instead *buy* the sailboats and the businessman would have to promise to buy it from the bank at a higher price in the future. As I have already mentioned, the increase in price is justified by the bank owning the sailboats, and therefore assuming responsibility for them, in the interim.

D. Bai'muajjal

This investment activity tool is equivalent to a deferred payment financing. Here, the financial institution purchases the contract for property or goods on a deferred payment schedule and then resells the property or goods to the customer. The financial institution pays the supplier on a progressive schedule, and the customer pays the institution through installments on the progressive schedule. Here as well it appears that the financial institution is interposing a form of riba; however, since the nature of the transaction is trading rather than lending, the reselling at a higher price is justified.

E. Ijara

Ijara is a lease transaction in which the financial institution purchases goods, usually machinery or equipment, and leases it to the customer. The customer would pay the institution a rental fee for a set period; if the customer wishes to purchase the good before or after the period, he may do so.

It is important to note that in the Islamic form of lease transaction, the lease begins at the date in which the goods are delivered to the customer, that the customer is not liable for the goods if they are destroyed, and that if there is a purchase of the goods at the end of the lease period, the contract cannot be made binding. These stipulations are different from conventional lease transactions (i.e., in conventional lease transactions, the beginning of the lease date is the date of the contract).

F. Bai'salam

Bai'salam is a transaction in which the entrepreneur sells his goods to a bank at a price determined in advance of delivery. Therefore, the bank sells the goods to the customer at a price determined during the formation of the contract, and the goods are delivered at a later date.

VIII. Recent Developments

The world's 1.2 billion Muslims are increasingly insisting that their money be invested according to Islamic principles[44]. With the phenomenon of globalization, international investors and businesses are struck with the need to cooperate with Islamic banking laws. The International Organization of Securities Commissions report annual growth of up to 20 percent during the past decade for the Islamic banking, insurance, and capital markets[45]. It also predicts that as much as half of the savings of the world's 1.3 billion Muslims will be in Islamic financial institutions by the year 2015.[46] The following table and map prepared by the IOSCO Task Force highlight the growth of the Islamic financial industry since its inception:

Stages of Evolution of the Islamic Financial Services Industry

1970s	1980s	1990s	2000s
Institutions: – Commercial Islamic Banks	**Institutions:** – Commercial Islamic Banks – Takaful – Islamic Investment Companies	**Institutions:** – Commercial Islamic Banks – Takaful – Islamic Investment Companies – Brokers/Dealers	**Institutions:** – Commercial Islamic Banks – Takaful – Islamic Investment Companies – Islamic Investment banks – Assets management Companies – E-commerce – Brokers/Dealers
Products: – Commercial Islamic Banking Products	**Products:** – Commercial banking products – Takaful	**Products:** – Commercial banking Products – Takaful – Mutual Funds/Unit Trust – Islamic Bonds – Shariah-complaint stocks	**Products:** – Commercial Banking Products – Takaful
Area: – Gulf/Middle East	**Area:** – Gulf/Middle East – Asia pacific		

Contd...

Contd...			
		– Islamic stockbroking **Area:** – Gulf/Middle East – Asia pacific	– Mutual Funds/Unit Trust – Islamic bonds – Shari 'a-complaint stocks – Islamic stockbroking
			Area: – Gulf/Middle East – Asia pacific - Europe/Americas – Global Offshore Market

Geographical Spread of Countries Using Shari'a-Compliant Procedures[47]

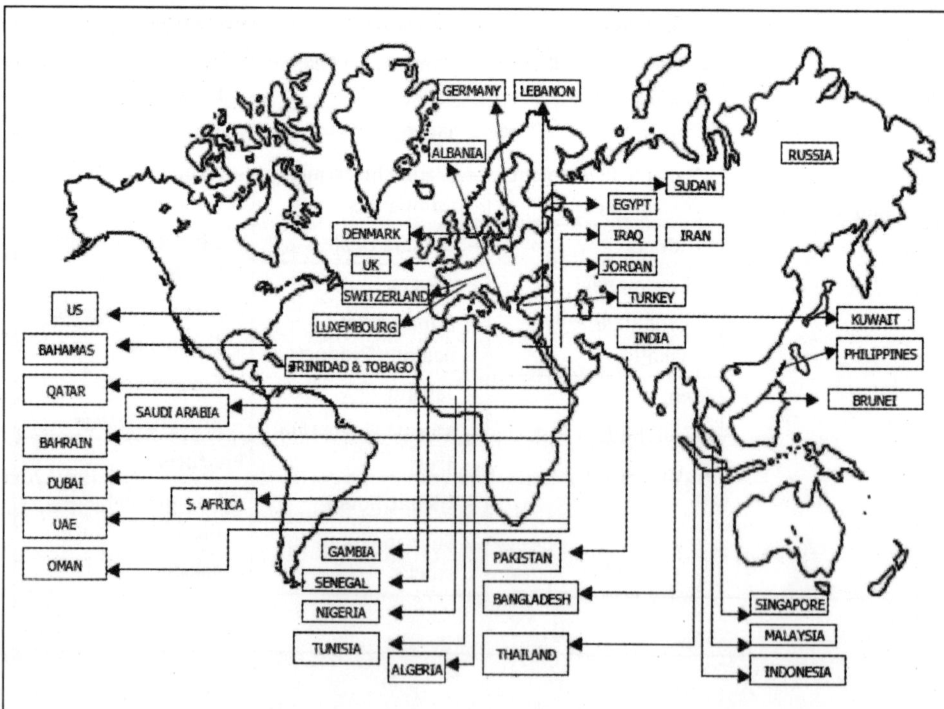

Today, Islamic banking is the most developed component of the Islamic financial system, and Islamic banks represent the bulk of the Islamic financial institutions worldwide[48]. The first recognized interest-free commercial bank was the Nasser Social Bank, established in Cairo, Egypt in 1971. With the goals of promoting the social economic progress of member countries and the use of Islamic finance worldwide, the Organization of the Islamic Conference founded the Islamic Development Bank (IDB). The creation of the IDB acted as a catalyst for the emergence of multiple banks in various countries: In 1975, the Dubai Islamic Bank; in 1977, the Faisal Islamic Bank of Egypt, the Faisal Islamic Bank of Sudan, and the Kuwait Finance House. Rapidly, Islamic banks were established across Asia and in Europe: The Bank Islam Malaysia Bhd in 1983 and the Islamic Bank International in Denmark in 1981.

Currently, there are estimated to be over 256 Islamic banks; total assets are estimated at USD 262 billion and the financial investments are above USD 400 billion. Deposits in Islamic banks are estimated to be over USD 202 billion worldwide and the average annual growth rate of the Islamic banking industry is ranged between 10-20% over the past decade[49]. Essentially, Islamic banks were established parallel to conventional banks. While some countries, as previously mentioned, have instituted Islamic banks, many conventional banks offer banking services based on Shari 'a principles. These components of conventional banks are known as "Islamic windows," which are often directed by Shari 'a advisors to oversee day-to-day operations. The great global banks— HSBC, Citibank, Deutsche Bank, Standard Chartered, and more— all have either Islamic windows or Islamic subsidiaries[50]. The following is an example of how Deutsche Bank has adopted Shari 'a compliant measures: Since it would be unlawful to issue bonds, or *sukuk* for a promise of a fixed rate of return, the Islamic subsidiary has mandated that the bond have an underlying asset backing it, where the bonds represent an equity asset rather than a loan[51].

These Islamic windows have also become popular for regional banks. In the US, for instance, regional banks like the University Bank in Michigan and the Devon Bank in Chicago have Islamic windows, with the former now having a full-fledged Islamic subsidiary[52]. The overall effect of Islamic windows and Islamic subsidiaries is the expansion of market capacity and innovation[53].

Investment funds are another area which has become Shari 'a compliant and expanded globally. These funds include property and realty funds, murabahah funds, and ijarah funds. Property and realty funds have recently become particularly popular in Europe and the Middle East. Between 1994 and the end of 2001, approximately 120 Islamic funds have been launched by both Islamic and conventional institutions[54]. Additionally, the IOSCO reports that Islamic equity funds grew at a rate of 25% between 1987 and 1994.[55] Today, one of the largest global financial institutions, JP Morgan Chase, has established an Islamic subsidiary to meet the requirements of Shari 'a.

IX. Impact of Current Islamic Practices and Failure to be Shari'a-Compliant

The desire for Shari 'a compliant measures was fueled by 1) the need to adhere to the mandates of religious doctrines such as the Qur'an and the Sunna and 2) to fulfill the social justice principles enshrined and envisioned in these religious doctrines. Non-Islamic financial institutions responded to this need by implementing Islamic windows and subsidiaries, which has rapidly expanded globally. The key inquiry, therefore, which is addressed in this thesis, is whether the use of alternative banking procedures has actually promoted the goals of Islamic law. In other words, has the use of Shari 'a-compliant measures provided for the greater good of society and aided in the reduction of poverty? Many experts hold that Islamic financial practices are even riskier than conventional practices and that they remain options only for the wealthy.

A. Theoretical Problems with Currently Proposed Tools

The earlier hypothetical about murabaha exemplifies the potential high risk. In this hypothetical, the businessman and the bank are involved in a murabaha transaction, whereby the bank purchases the sailboats for the businessman to later purchase at a higher price. The problem here is that "there is no minimum time interval for the bank to own the property before selling it with the markup."[56] Some scholars argue that the typical time interval is extremely small and the bank transfers ownership to the client immediately. As murabaha is asset-based, it would be very difficult for a businessman who needs a working-capital loan. The businessman would need cash from the bank to meet expenses for starting the business and a bank would only grant this money in exchange for equity interest in the business. Such a system would be risky for the bank and thus hard to obtain on the part of the businessman.

Experts opine that every Islamic bank has at least three-quarters of its investments structured as murabaha. Even the inaptly named Islamic Development Bank was, as of the mid-1980s, doing four-fifths of its business through murabaha, and only 1 percent through equity transactions[57]. If this is the case, then most financial transactions would appear to serve wealthier entrepreneurs rather than helping the poor. Theoreticians or Islamic economists now urge that the Shari 'a-compliant system can only meet the social justice objectives if it not only excludes the mandates prohibited in Islam, but if it *includes* those recommended by religion.

The mode of mudaraba as well, has been strongly criticized. Islamic theorists argue that the replacement of pre-determined interest by uncertain profits can be just as exploitative as interest if it is excessive. It has also been argued that historically, mudaraba enabled women and the aged to engage in trade through merchants for a share in the profits, where all losses were borne by the owners of capital[58]. An inequitable allocation of risk would render mudaraba in violation of Qur'anic precepts.

B. Case Studies

Many case studies analyze the Islamic banking systems operating in Egypt, Sudan, Malaysia, and Pakistan. The primary problem identified by the case studies is the high rate of borrower delinquency[59]. In practice, murahaba payments have often been held up because late payments cannot be penalized under this system. In response, Pakistani banks have employed a "mark-down" practice of giving rebates as an incentive for early payment[60]. This system functions as a form of interest and its legitimacy is debatable.

A case study of the Phillipine Amanah Bank by Mastura highlights other concerns. First, the PAB is a bank that operates by providing both interest on deposits as well as interest-free deposits through Islamic windows. The critique of this form of operation is that the institution is not truly Islamic if it incorporates both practices, especially as it focuses mostly on murabaha transactions as opposed to the mudaraba and musharaka means of financing. Secondly, this PAB also dealt with excess liquidity by making use of interest-bearing treasury bills[61]. The study amply illustrates that financial institutions attempt to be Shari 'a-compliant, yet use indirect forms of interest.

X. Different Interpretation of Riba is Necessary

The "interest-free" financial structures described in Part V attain the same result as a conventional "interest bearing" banking structure. In each one, the borrower has little savings and must pay an amount that is above the nominal cost of the loan. In the name of risk sharing, and by incorporating a middleman or indirect path, the methods allow the lenders still to receive a premium. The premium is not labeled as "interest," but still performs the same definitive role.

Ostensibly, the result of this banking structure is not only that it violates the Qur'anic injunctions and the narratives of Muhammad's words and acts, but it fails to fulfill the social justice principles of equitable wealth distribution envisioned in the sources in the first place. In order to resolve this problem, I propose that there are two primary options available: 1) Maintain the current Islamic banking structures and modify it such that it could possibly reduce the additional amount burdened on the borrower or 2) reinterpret riba such that it is consistent with the words of the Qur'an and the principles underlying them. I argue that the first option would not fully redress the problems of Islamic banking. Even if financing tools are altered such that they are more equitable, they will nonetheless incorporate indirect forms of interest. I urge that a reinterpretation of riba is necessary to avoid hypocrisy.

Redefining riba would accomplish the goals of both adhering to the Islamic law mandates as well as providing a greater opportunity of achieving equitable distribution of wealth. I believe that a moderate interest rate does not qualify as the unjustified or exorbitant increase in price that the Qur'an refers to. One illustration of this interpretation is given by the Hanbali school of thought. The Hanbali school suggests a modest interest rate, one that is less than or equal to the rate of inflation[62]. Thus, at the date of repayment, the interest rate specified in the contract is compared to the prevailing interest rate. This increase will be permitted since it would simply maintain the real value of the capital sum, without "any usurious sums extracted beyond the real value of the capital by examining each transaction retrospectively."[63]

While I believe that several interpretations of riba are conceivable, I propose that in the very least the following rationales would render better solutions than the Classical view: 1) maintenance of the real value of capital is permitted and anything beyond it would be outlawed (as suggested by the Hanbali school; 2) any form of interest that is not exorbitant is necessary for the greater good[64]; and 3) money and interest are newer concepts and outside the scope of riba altogether, (because the only forms of currency outlawed by the Qur'an were gold and silver), and therefore permissible.

One potential argument with the moderate use of interest is that the Islamic institution would then be no different from the Western institution. The response is that the two forms of institutions would be inherently distinct because their underlying ideologies are fundamentally different, and thus the interest would be used to achieve different goals. Under the Islamic framework, profit is used to achieve a spiritual end, and a more centralized governmental power to guide the choice of businesses. The capitalist system, however, seeks profit as an end itself. Moreover, there is vast discretion of individual choice and highly decentralized government in attaining this end. Differences are further underscored through Shari 'a mandates other than the prohibition of riba. As mentioned in Part V, the banking system further proscribes activities considered haram, which include gambling and the alcohol beverage trade. Despite these differences, the use of interest and common desire of attaining profit permit the compatibility of both systems.

XI. Conclusion

The growth of Islamic banking is symptomatic of the global demand of Shari 'a- compliant products. This growth illustrates not only the desire to follow the religious mandates and the spirit of Islam, but the social economic capabilities of such a popular system. The current tools are inadequate to fulfill such desires and expectations and provide some difficulty in becoming compatible with the Western banking system. I argue that the only solution would be to provide a moderate form of interest. As a matter of Islamic law, this could only be achieved by a second consensus to the change the prevailing interpretation of riba. While some countries *do* endorse alternative views, as opposed to the Classical view, a second consensus will render a uniform agreement of the boundaries of riba and provide a powerful movement towards a more equitable distribution of wealth.

(Sapana Shah, 2304 Jefferson Square Court, Decatur, GA 30030. The author can be reached at skshah5@emory.edu).

Endnotes

1 Sami Zubaida, Law and Power in the Islamic World, The Shari' a and Political Aurhority 1-27 (2005).

2 42 Mohammed El Qorchi, International Monetary Fund, Islamic Finance Gears Up, Finance and Development Magazine, International Monetary Fund (2005), *http://www.imf.org/external/pubs/ft/fandd/2005/12/qorchi.htm.*

3 Id.

4 Id.

5 Hesham M. Sharawy, Note: Understanding the Islamic Prohibition of Interest: A Guide to Aid Economic Cooperation Between the Islamic and Western Worlds, 29 GA. J. INT'L & COMP. L. 154-58 (2000).

6 Khaled Abou El Fadl, Article: The Place of Ethical Obligations in Islamic Law, 4 UCLA J. ISLAMIC & NEAR E.L. 1-5 (2004/2005).

7 Id. at 5.

8 Id.

9 Id.

10 Michael J. Taylor, Article: Islamic Banking- The Feasibility of Establishing an Islamic Bank in the United States, 40 AM. BUS. L.J. 387 (2003).

11 Id.

12 Mahmoud A. El-Gamal, 'Interest' and the Paradox of Contemporary Islamic Law and Finance, *http://www.ruf.rice.edu/~elgamal/files/interest.pdf.*

13 Sharawy, supra note 5 at 160.

14 Id.

15 Chian Wu, Note: Islamic Banking: Signs of Sustainable Growth, 16 MINN. J. INT'L L. 233-237 (2007).

16 Id.

17 Id.

18 Id.

19 Id.

20 Mohamed Ariff, Islamic Banking, Asian-Pacific Economic Literature (1988), *http://www.usc.edu/dept/MSA/economics/islamic_banking.html.*

21 Id.

22 Id.

23 Qur'an, II:276

24 Taylor, supra note 10.

25 Ariff, supra note 20.

26 Id.

27 Id.

28 Qur'an, III:130

29 Barbara L. Seniawski, Notes: Riba Today: Social Equity, the Economy, and Doing Business Under Islamic Law, 39 Colum. J. Transnat'L L. 701 (2001).

30 Id.

31 Jean-Francois Seznec, Special Feature: Global Financial Reform, Ethics, Islamic Banking and the Global Financial Market, 23 FLETCHER F. WORLD AFF. 161, 163 (1999).

32 Id.

33 Id.

34 Umar F. Moghul, Esq., Arshad A. Ahmed, Esq., Fourteenth Annual Philip D. Reed Memorial Issue: Islam and the Law: Contemporary Views and Perspectives: Islamic Law and Finance: Article: Contractual Forms in Islamic Finance Law and Islamic Inv. Co. Of the Gulf (Bahamas) Ltd. V. Symphony Gems N.V. & Ors.: A First Impression of Islamic Finance, 27 FORDHAM INT'L L.J. 150 (2003).

35 Id.

36 Id. While the prohibition of gharar is a significant aspect of Shari 'a-compliant structures, I focus more on the interpretation of riba in my thesis. I argue that a reinterpretation of riba is first necessary for compliance with Islamic precepts.

37 Kent Benedict Gravelle, Islamic Law in Sudan: A Comparative Analysis, ILSA J. INT'L & COMP. L. 1, 19 (1998).

38 Kuwait Commercial Code, Law No. 68, Art. 115 (1980).

39 Dr. S. E. Rayner,The Theory of Contracts in Islamic Law: A Comparative Analysis with Particular Reference to the Modern Legislation in Kuwait, Bahrain and the United Arab Emirates, 281 (1991).

40 Seznec, supra note 25.

41 Id.

42 Id.

43 S.H. Amin, Islamic Banking and Finance: The Experience of Iran, 15 (1986).

44 Will Rasmussen, Islamic Finance Demand Rising, But Depth Lacking, Reuters, March 27, 2007.

45 International Organization of Securities Commissions, Report of the Islamic Capital Market Task Force of the International Organization of Securities Commissions, Islamic Capital Market Fact Finding Report (2004), *http://www.iosco.org/library/pubdocs/pdf/IOSCOPD170.pdf.*

46 Id.

47 Id at 16.

48 Id at 22.

49 Id at 27.

50 Abdulkader Thomas, Islamic Finance Goes Global, Far Eastern Economic Review (March 2007), *http://www.feer.com/articles1/2007/0703/free/islamicf.html.*

51 Aaron Maclean, Islamic Banking: Is It Really Kosher? American.Com Magazine, (March/April 2007), *http://www.american.com/archive/2007/march-april-magazine-contents/islamic-banking-is-it-really-kosher.*

52 Id.

53 Id.

54 Id.

55 Id.

56 Id.

57 Id.

58 Id.

59 Mohamed Ariff, Islamic Banking, Asian-Pacific Economic Literature (1988), *http://www.usc.edu/dept/MSA/economics/islamic_banking.html.*

60 Id.

61 Id.

62 Seniawski, supra note 24 at 711

63 Id.

64 Id.

5

Banking for the Poor

The Role of Islamic Banking in Microfinance Initiatives

Asyraf Wajdi Dusuki

Purpose – The main purpose of this paper is to review the microfinance scheme and discuss how Islamic banks can participate in such endeavour without actually compromising on the issue of institutional viability and sustainability.

Design/methodology/approach – The paper is based an extensive review of microfinance with the objectives to build a case for Islamic banking to participate in microfinance initiative.

Findings – As reviewed in this paper, microfinance requires innovative approaches beyond the traditional financial intermediary role. Among others, building human capacity through social intermediation and designing group-based lending programmes are proven to be among the effective tools to reduce transaction costs and lower

Source: Asyraf Wajdi Dusuki, Humanomics: The International Journal of Systems and Ethics, Issue 1, Volume 24, pp 49-66,

exposure to numerous financial risks in relation to providing credit to the rural poor. This paper also suggests the use of special purpose vehicle, SPV as one of the possible alternatives for Islamic banks channelling funds to the poor.

Research limitations/implications – Islamic banks may benefit from spectrum of Shari 'ah-compliant sources of funds and offer a wide array of financing instruments catering to different needs and demands of their clients. Furthermore, the use of a bankruptcy-remote entity like SPV can protect Islamic banks from any adverse effect of microfinance activities.

Originality/Value – The analysis here is valuable in drawing attention to Islamic banking practitioners that they can actually practise microfinance without undermining their institutional viability, competitiveness and sustainability. This is evident from the proposed model to incorporate Special Purpose Vehicle (SPV) into their microfinance initiatives.

1. Introduction

Attacking persistent poverty and overcoming low levels of social and economic development of Muslims worldwide are the greatest challenges in facing the global development community as the world has already moved into the new millennium. Despite progress during the last three decades witnessing a revolution in providing finance for alleviating poverty across the globe, the battle is far from won. Consequently, the issue of financial inclusion has emerged as a policy concern primarily to ensure provision of credit to small and medium enterprises that are normally denied access to credit mainstream financial institutions and market. The emerging microfinance revolution with appropriate designed financial products and services enable the poor to expand and diversify their economic activities, increase their incomes and improve their social well-being (Bennett & Cuevas, 1996; Ledgerwood, 1999).

The concern over poverty reduction via microfinance initiative is also of relevance to Islamic banks. As business entity established within the ambit of *Shariah* (Islamic law),

Islamic banks are expected to be guided by an Islamic economic objectives, among others, to ensure that wealth is fairly circulated among as many hands as possible without causing any harm to those who acquired it lawfully (Ibn Ashur, 2006). Indeed, Islamic banking industry is one of the fastest growing industries, having posted double-digit annual growth rates for almost 30 years (Iqbal & Molyneux, 2005). What started as a small rural banking experiment in the remote villages of Egypt in the early 1970s, has now reached a level where many mega-international banks worldwide offering Islamic banking products. While the estimates about the exact magnitude of the Islamic banking market vary, one can safely assume that it presently exceeds USD 150 billion and is poised for further growth (Iqbal & Molyneux, 2005).

With such an impressive growth of Islamic banking over the last 30 years, this paper argues that it is time for the industry to be reoriented to emphasize on issues relating to social and economic ends of financial transactions, rather than overemphasizing on making profits and meeting the bottom line alone. Islamic banks should endeavour to be the epicentre in the financial business galaxy of promoting financial inclusive by engaging with community banking and microfinance programme.

This paper reviews the evolution of microfinance industry with the objectives to build a case for Islamic banking to participate without jeopardising their viability and sustainability in the market. The remaining of this paper is organised as follows. Next section delineates some theoretical issues on the existing numerous barriers to finance the poor, Section 3 discusses the potential of microfinance in enforcing social intermediation role and group-based lending mechanism to overcome such barriers. Section 4 discusses the relevance of microfinance initiatives to Islamic banking. Section 5 then highlights the potential of special purpose vehicle or SPV as an alternative approach for Islamic banks to practice microfinance without compromising with the issue of viability and sustainability. Fittingly, the conclusion is in the final section.

2. Barriers in Banking for the Poor

It is well established in finance theory that credit markets characterized with high asymmetric information, notably, the existence of moral hazard and adverse selection problems, leads to severe distortion and sometimes complete collapse of the formal credit market (Akerlof, 1970; Daripa, 2000). Financial contracts will not be written under this condition; hence goods and services will be underproduced and underconsumed.

The contracts between borrower and lender will only be honoured if the element of trust exists in such transactions. The basis of trust depends on two critical elements; first is the applicant's reputation as a person of honour (Diamond, 1991) and; second is the availability of enough capital or collateral against which claims can be made in case of default (Holmstrom & Tirole, 1993).

The essence of conventional profit-maximization banks as financial intermediaries providing financial services to people hinge upon these two elements. As formal lenders, risk-averse banks would only be willing to lend if these two elements serving as a basis of trust exist in their reciprocal relationship with clients (as borrowers). For instance, the bank is able to assess the reputation of borrowers based on bank's intimate knowledge embedded in the clients personal accounts as well as other documented history of past borrower behaviour. At the same time, the clients have material value such as properties or any valuable assets serving as collateral to pledge against risk.

However, these two elements poised important impediments to the poor especially in the rural areas to access into credit market. The poor are usually perceived by the 'profit-orientated' banks as high-risk borrowers due to inherent difficulties in assessing their creditworthiness, at the same time their inability to provide collateral to pledge against any potential risk.

These traditional formal lenders faced with borrowers whom they do not personally know, who do not keep written accounts or 'business plans' and who want to borrow small and uneconomic sums (Jacklen, 1988); thus exposing them to very high risks due to the inherent screening problems faced by the lenders at the same time make the project appraisal become too expensive (Rhyne & Otero, 1992).

Most formal intermediaries like commercial banks also regard low-income households as 'too poor' to save, thus further accentuates the risk of supplying credits to them (Adams & Vogel, 1986; Sinclair, 1998). Furthermore, no insurer is willing to insure against possibility of nonrepayment due to natural and commonest hazards afflicting small producers in developing countries; for example, drought, livestock disease and breakdown of equipment (Hulme & Mosley, 1996). The risk exposure in supplying credits to the poor clients is further exacerbated due to the inherent difficulty for the commercial financial institution to diversify their portfolio. For example, most of the rural clients who derive their incomes from agriculture need to borrow in the pre-harvest season, making it difficult for banks to diversify their portfolio (Zeller & Sharma, 1998).

Both financial institutions and poor clients face high transaction costs due to asymmetric information problems which naturally appear in the financial transactions. These costs related to searching, monitoring and enforcement costs which are directly related to the information problems inherent in the rural financial markets. The uncertainty regarding the ability of borrowers to meet future loan obligations, inability to monitor the use of funds and demand for small sum of loans by the rural households further reinforces the higher units of transaction costs, which is characterised by fixed costs[1] (Braverman & Guasch, 1986; Zeller & Meyer, 2002).

Likewise, physical and socio-economic barriers may also contribute to the market failure. These include poor infrastructure, remote, difficult terrain and stagnant, illiteracy, poor healthcare, malnutrition, caste or ethnicity and gender (Bennett, Goldberg, & Hunte, 1996). These barriers are more apparent in developing countries whereby over 90% of households living in the rural areas are without access to institutional sources of finance (Robinson, 2001). Thus, matching access to or supply of financial services with demand has been a consistent challenge for financial institutions attempting to serve clientele groups outside the frontier of formal finance (J. D. Von Pischke, 1991).

Figure 1 depicts the common factors faced and perceived by both the supply side (formal financial intermediation) and the demand side (the poor) resulting in the financial market failure for the poor.

3. Evolution of Microfinance

The failure of commercial banking to provide financial services to the poor coupled with disadvantages of using informal markets are major rationales for intervention in the market for financial services at the micro level. Consequently, microfinance emerged as an economic development approach intended to address the financial needs of the deprived groups in the society. The term microfinance refers to "the provision of financial services to low-income clients, including self-employed, low-income entrepreneurs in both urban and rural areas" (Ledgerwood, 1999).

Figure 1: Factors that Affect Financial Market Failures for the Poor

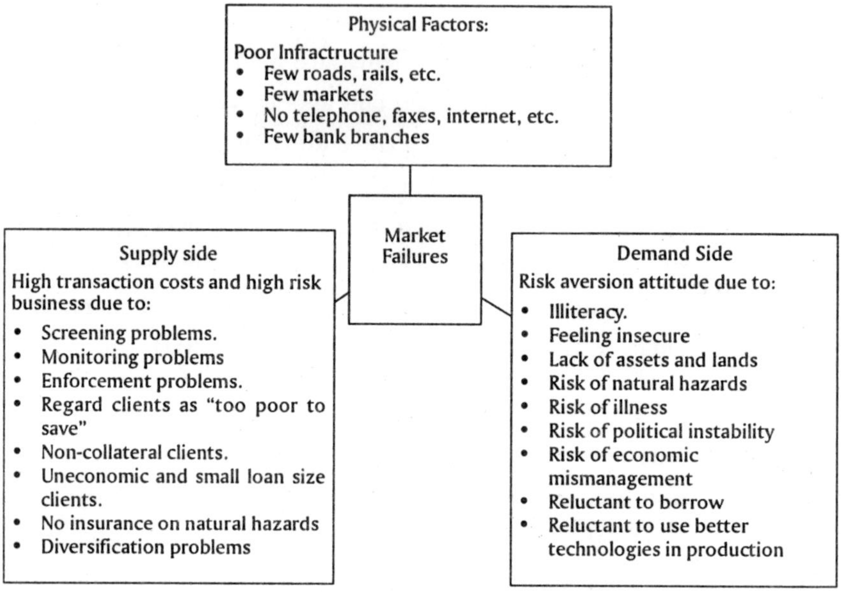

The emergence of this new paradigm was encouraged by the successful story of microfinance innovations serving the poor throughout 1970s and 1980s. The most quoted examples are Grameen Bank Bangladesh, the *unit desa* system of Bank Rakyat Indonesia, ACCION International in United States and Latin America and PRODEM, BancoSol's predecessor in Bolivia. The microfinance adopts market-oriented and enterprise development approach. It emphasises institutional and programme innovations to reduce costs and risks and has greater potential to expand the financial frontier to the poor in sustainable manner (Littlefield, Morduch, & Hashemi, 2003).

The following highlights some salient features of microfinance mechanism.

1. Integrating Social Intermediation

Providing financial services to marginalised society often requires more than traditional style of financial intermediation. Financing the poor entails some measures of up-front investment to nurture human capacity (e.g., knowledge, skills, confidence and information) and build local institutions as a bridge to reduce gaps created by poverty, illiteracy, gender and remoteness (Ledgerwood, 1999). This process of building capacity among the marginalised society is known in microfinance literature as social intermediation.

Thus, social intermediation is defined as "a process in which investments are made in the development of both human resources and institutional capital, with the aim of increasing self-reliance of marginalised groups, preparing them to engage in formal financial intermediation" (Bennett *et al.*, 1996; Pitt & Khandker, 1996). Social intermediation is different from other common types of social welfare services because it offers mechanism enabling beneficiaries to become clients who should then ready to enter into a contract involving reciprocal obligations. This aspect of social intermediation should eventually prepare individuals to enter into solid business relationships with formal financial institutions. The process normally involves training members in basic accounting and financial management as well as business strategy to ensure viability and sustainability of financial services offered. Figure 2 illustrates the process of social intermediation in microfinance initiatives aiming at preparing groups to enter into solid business relationship (a contract involving reciprocal obligations) with formal financial institutions.

Figure 2: The Process of Social Intermediation

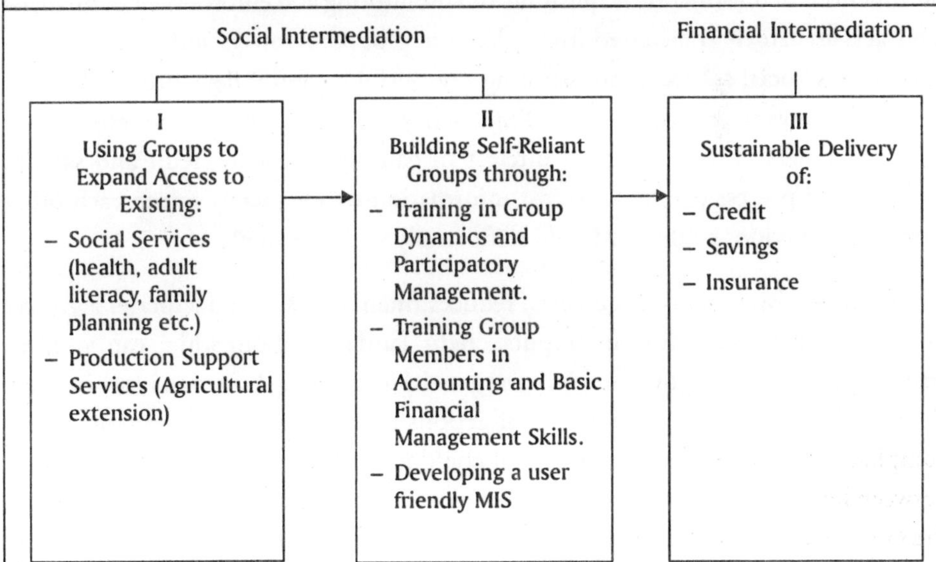

Sources: Bennett et al., 1996

By playing the role of social intermediation, bank is not only building self-reliant groups of poor people in rural areas with related skills that could foster long-term business relationship but also exploiting cost advantage of informal monitoring and enforcement systems in the long-run which is inevitably important for a more efficient and effective role of financial intermediation.

2. Group-based Financial Services

Many successful microfinance initiatives worldwide adopt group-based lending approach capitalising on peer monitoring and guarantee mechanism. Group-based approach normally involves the formation of groups of people who have a common objective to access financial services. One important feature of group-based lending is the use of peer pressure as a substitute to collateral. It has been proven empirically as one of the most effective ways of designing an incentive-monitoring system in the presence of costly information[2].

Another important feature of group-based lending mechanism is its potential to reduce transaction costs in credit delivery and disbursements (searching, monitoring and enforcement) of the lender by shifting onto the groups. Within such systems, the functions of information acquisition and monitoring and enforcement of financial contracts are largely transferred from a bank to group borrowers and savers[3]. It may also harness 'social collateral' constituting a powerful incentive device to yield higher repayment rates than individual lending (Besley & Coate, 1995). The self-selected group members share a common interest in gaining access to credit and savings services, and possess enough low-cost information to adequately screen each other and apply sanctions to those who do not comply with the rule[4].

Hence, it lowers transaction costs, reduces financial risk and facilitates a greater range of market transactions in outputs, credit, land and labour which can, in turn, lead to better incomes. For example, strong social link among borrowers may increase their ability to participate in credit transactions characterized by uncertainty about compliance[5]. In particular, social capital could lead to a better flow of information between lenders and borrowers and hence less adverse selection and moral hazard in the credit market. Social capital also potentially expands the range of enforcement mechanisms for default on obligations in environments in which recourse to the legal system is costly or impossible. Again, trust (social capital) plays a paramount role in the formation of group lending success, particularly in the absence of collateral. (Besley & Coate, 1995; Bhatt & Tang, 1998; Collier, 1998; Krishna, Uphoff, & Esman, 1997; Narayan & Pritchett, 1999; Otero & Rhyne, 1994; Stiglitz, 1990; Zeller & Sharma, 1998).

3. Savings Mobilization

Savings are also regarded crucial in building self-sufficient microfinance institutions. Saving mobilization can strengthen microfinance institutions and reduce their dependence on government subsidies and donors for loanable funds (Gurgad, Pederson, & Yaron, 1994; J.D. Von Pischke, Adams, & Donald, 1986; Rhyne & Otero, 1992; 1994). Well-crafted saving services can encourage a move from non-financial savings into financial savings, with advantages for entrepreneurs of safety and liquidity and for society of providing funds for investment by others (Vogel, 1984). For example, Grameen Bank, Amanah Ikhtiar Malaysia and several programmes of ACCION International have used some form of compulsory savings, where borrowers are required to save a portion of the amount they borrow.

The amount required for compulsory savings is sometimes determined based on a percentage of the loan granted or sometimes as a nominal amount. For example, in the case of Amanah Ikhtiar Malaysia, participants who signed as a member but yet to borrow are required to save RM1 per week as a compulsory saving and an amount between RM3 to RM15 for borrowers depending on the loan size. A distinctive characteristic of compulsory savings is that the funds cannot be withdrawn by members while they have a loan outstanding. In this way, savings act as a form of collateral and serve as an additional guarantee mechanism to ensure repayment of loans. On the other hand BRI Unit Desa System in Indonesia offers a voluntary savings instruments such as passbook savings, with free access to deposits, which better meets depositors' liquidity requirements.

4. Over-dependence on Subsidies

There is also a growing debate on the need for microfinance institutions to be independence from subsidy or self-sufficient. Several shortcomings have been identified in the microfinance literature with regards to over-dependence on subsidies. Among the arguments include—subsidies can cause a lack of financial discipline on the part of both lender and borrower. While the lenders may have less concern about repayment rates, borrowers on the hand perceived loan as grants which may reduce their sense of obligation to repay their debts (Bennett *et al.,* 1996). Low and subsidized interest rates also have been empirically proven to result in regressive income distribution, credit rationing and non-sustainable institution (Gurgad *et al.,* 1994). Furthermore, the infusions of subsidies may induce entry and lead to perverse effects to borrowers' welfare in the face of stiff competition among the unregulated moneylenders. (Hoff & Stiglitz, 1998).[6]

Therefore, there is mounting concern that financial services can be sold to the poor without recurrent subsidies under conditions that allow the financial intermediary to become self-sustainable. One of the alternatives is to respond directly to the World Bank's long-standing concern about economic rationality of credit project interest rates (J.D. Von Pischke, 1996). Appropriate interest rate charged is one that will allow social banking institution to cover its operating costs without further reliance on subsidies and donor funds. One of the important components in calculating appropriate interest rates besides the costs (including inflation rate) to be covered is profit, as measured by the capitalization rate. However, this component of charging interest on microfinance product is not feasible for Islamic banks to emulate since it violates the fundamental principle of Shari'ah which we are going to discuss in the folowing section.

4. Islamic Banking Approach to Microfinance

Concern over credit provision and finance accessibility for the poor via microfinance is also relevant to Islamic banks that should place greater social welfare responsibilities and religious commitments to achieve the Islamic economic objectives, including social justice, equitable distribution of income and wealth and promoting economic development. Many writers such as El-Gamal (2006), Al-Harran (1990, 1996, 1999), Akhtar (1996, 1998), Dhumale and Sapcanin (1998), Ahmed (2001), and others, believe in the great potential of Islamic banking to be involved in microfinance programmes to cater for the needs of the poor who usually fall outside the formal banking sector.

In fact the earliest Islamic banking experiments in India and Egypt were small rural co-operatives inspired by European mutuals. The institution such as Mit Ghamr in Egypt had focused on economic development, poverty alleviation and fostering a culture of thrift among poor Muslims. However, with the passage of time, the orientation of Islamic banking and finance has somehow dominated by profit-maximisation doctrine, vying for countless billions of Arab petrodollars. As a result, most of the financial engineered instruments are designed favorably catering the needs of the well-off clients while the poor left unbankable due to the inherent impediments as discussed earlier.

Perhaps this phenomenon does not reflect the raison-d'-etre of Islamic banking which is supposed to be a Shariah-based institution. As the name suggests, Islamic banking is first and foremost about religious identity and duty. There are fundamental differences between Islamic banks and their conventional counterparts, not only in the ways they practice their business, as argued by the advocates of Islamic banking, but above all in the values which guide the Islamic banks' whole operation and outlook (K. Ahmad, 2000; Z. Ahmad, 1984; M. Umar Chapra, 1987; M. Umer Chapra, 2000b; Khan & Mirakhor, 1987; Rosly & Bakar, 2003; Siddiqi, 1983, 1985; Siddiqui, 2001). The values as prevailed within the ambit of Shariah are expressed not only in the minutiae of their transactions, but in the breadth of their role in society as a manifestation of religious belief and a commitment to addressing the issue of income inequality, poverty eradication and social justice.

On the whole, Islamic banking is concerned with much more than just refraining from charging interest. It is a system that aims at making a positive contribution to the fulfilment of the socioeconomic objectives of Islamic society inscribed in Maqasid al-Shariah (the objectives of Shariah). As business entity established within the ambit of Shariah, Islamic banks are expected to be guided by an Islamic economic objectives, among others, to ensure that wealth is fairly circulated among as many hands as possible without causing any harm to those who acquired it lawfully (Ibn Ashur, 2006). Hence the issue of financing the poor via microfinance initiative is not alien to Islamic banking. Instead it is a natural outlook that should transpire in the operation of any Islamic institution, especially those claiming to be based on the principles of Shariah.

While Islamic banks may emulate the existing model of microfinance practice, the activities however must be carried out in ways which do not conflict with the principles of Shariah. In other words, Islamic microfinance initiatives should be free from any involvement of activities prohibited by Islam and from elements like usury (*riba*), gambling (*maisir*), harmful substance (*darar*) and excessive ambiguity (*gharar*). Having mentioned this, Islamic banks can always learn from various approaches used by microfinance institutions to ensure effectiveness in providing finance to the marginalized society.

In addition to the innovative approaches used by many microfinance institutions, Islamic banking can apply diverse financial instruments together with other available mechanisms such as *zakah*, charity and *waqf* which can be integrated into microfinance programmes to promote entrepreneurship amongst the poor and subsequently alleviate poverty (Akhtar, 1996, 1998; S. Al-Harran, 1995, 1996, 1999; S. A. S. Al-Harran, 1990; Al-ZamZami & Grace, 2000; Dhumale & Sapcanin, 1998; Hassan & Alamgir, 2002).

The following sections delineate the various instruments in Islamic finance for mobilization of funds and financing the poor.

Mobilization of Funds

As noted earlier, conventional microfinance relies heavily on simple interest-based deposits, government subsidies, donations and loans. On the other hand, Islamic microfinance can benefit from a wide array of instruments for funds mobilization. Islamic microfinance instruments may be broadly divided into: (1) Internal Resources and (2) External Resources. The former relates to financial resources that can be mobilized internally to ensure self-sustainability and self-sufficiency, while the latter reflects the common practice of microfinance institutions worldwide which rely on external parties to provide financial resources like government grants, subsidies and donations. A brief description on the instruments for funds mobilization is discussed below:

(1) Internal Resources

The internal resources can be further divided into two main categories, namely deposits and equity. The following describes the salient characteristics of Islamic deposits and equity that can be mobilised for microfinance purposes.

1. Deposits

Islamic microfinance can mobilise various forms of deposits such as *wadiah* (safekeeping), *qard al-hassan* (benevolence loan) and *mudarabah* (profit sharing).

Under *wadiah* mechanism, the deposits are held as *amanah* (trust) and utilised by the bank at its own risk. The depositors are not entitled to any return since the profit or loss resulting from the investment of these funds is entirely belonged to the bank. However, bank can offer unilateral and discretionary gifts which sometimes commensurate to the rate of return given by conventional counterpart on its interest-bearing deposits. Another model is using *qard al hassan* mechanism, whereby the funds deposited in the bank is treated as a loan by the depositor. Here, bank shall have to guarantee the principal amount but is not allowed to offer any return to depositors. *Mudarabah* deposits on the other hand are based on profit sharing between the bank acting as the entrepreneur (*mudarib)* and depositors as the capital owner (*rabb-ul maal*). The amount deposited is not supposed to be guaranteed and depositors are entitled to any return derived from the invested funds.

2. Equity

Islamic microfinance initiative may also mobilise funds through participatory models such as *musharakah* and *mudarabah*. There is a great potential to attract depositors amongst the rich who intend to do charity via Islamic participatory approach of risk and profit-sharing. In *musharakah* model of fund-raising, public can buy shares and become owners of the whole microfinance programme initiated by Islamic banks or choose specific financing project of their choice. Any profits realised from the project are distributed annually to the shareholders. While losses incurred shall be shared proportionate to the amount of capital contributed by each participant. In this regard, Islamic banks guarantee the participation of every segment of society. In particular, the adoption of Islamic participatory approach in fund mobilization and financing promotes justice, brotherhood, social equality and financial inclusion as opposed to the emerging financial exclusion which is becoming a common phenomenon in most developed countries.

(2) External Resources

As mentioned earlier, conventional microfinance institutions charge high interest rate to allow them to cover their operating costs without further reliance on subsidies and donor funds. Islamic banks on the other hand are not allowed to charge interest and thus require alternative mechanisms for funds mobilization to preserve institutional financial sustainability. Islam offers mechanisms for redistribution of income and wealth and enhancement of social inclusion, so that every Muslim is guaranteed a fair standard of living (Metwally, 1997). These mechanisms include *zakah*, donations, gift and *waqf* are inherent in Islamic charitable contracts (*tabarru'*). *Zakah* is a compulsory religious levy which can be mobilised from Muslims and disbursed to the designated recipients as prescribed by *Shariah* (Al-Omar & Abdel-Haq, 1996). It can be used to resolve the issue of financing the poorest of the poor or hardcore poor who normally require certain amount of funds for their basic consumption purposes. In other words, *zakah* can be utilised for consumption needs of the poor while other types of funds shall be used for financing productive activities.

Waqf is a form of perpetual charity that entails the use of assets such as cash, land, real estates for charitable purposes. One of the unique characteristics of *waqf* instruments is its perpetuity that does not allow *waqf* asset to be disposed of and its ownership cannot be transferred. Thus *waqf* creates and preserves long-term assets that generates income flows or indirectly help the process of production and creation of wealth.

Demand-Oriented Financing

Impact studies on microfinance initiatives have shown that the effectiveness of microfinance in alleviating poverty depending on how sensitive the microfinance institution to client demand. The need to focus on demand-oriented financial services induces them to greater institutional and programmes innovation especially in products differentiation, operation efficiency and more outreach improvement. For instance, the scope of lending services offered to the poor must address not only production- and income-generating activities but also consumption needs such as health, education and social obligation. Consequently better financing products will generate greater economic benefits for poor clients and eventually larger impact to the society, particularly the poor (Seibel & Parhusip, 1998; Zeller & Meyer, 2002).

Accordingly, Islamic banks can offer a wide-array of *Shariah*-compliant financing instruments addressing various needs and demands of the client especially among the poor entrepreneur. These instruments can be broadly divided into: (1) participatory profit-loss-sharing modes like *mudarabah* and *musharakah*; (2) exchange (*muawadat*) modes like *murabahah* (cost plus sale), *bay' bithaman 'ajil* (deferred payment sale), *bay' al-Salam* (forward sale) and *bay' al-Istisna'* (commission to manufacture sale), *Ijarah* (leasing); (3) voluntary charitable contract (*tabarru'*), such as, pawning contract (*ar-Rahn*) and benevolence loan (*qard al-hassan*) and (4) hybridmodes like diminishing partnership (*musharakah mutanaqisah*), hire purchase (*ijarah thumma albay*) etc. A brief description of each financing instrument and its relevant application is provided in the following Table 1.

Table 1: Shariah-Compliant Financing Instruments for Microfinance

Category	Instrument	Description	Application
1.Participatory-based	Musharakah	A partnership contract between two parties who both contribute capital towards the financing of a project. Both parties share profits on a pre-agreed ratio, but losses are shared on the basis of equity participation. Either parties or just one of them may carry out management of the project. This is a very flexible partnership arrangement where the sharing of the profits and management can be negotiated and pre-agreed by all parties.	This financing mode is suitable for working capital financing, fixed asset purchased, project financing etc.
	Mudarabah	An agreement made between two parties: one which provides 100 percent of the capital for the project and another party known as a mudarrib, who manages the project using his entrepreneurial skills. Profits are distributed according to a predetermined ratio. Any losses accruing are borne by the provider of capital. The provider of capital has no control over the management of the project.	This financing mode is suitable for working capital financing, fixed asset purchased, project financing etc.

Contd...

Contd...			
2.Exchange-based (muawadat)	Murabahah	A contract sale between the bank and its client for the sale of goods at a price which includes a profit margin agree by both parties. As a financing technique, it involves the purchase of goods by the bank as requested by the client. The goods are sold to the client with a mark up. Repayment, usually in instalments is specified in the contract.	This financing mode is suitable for working capital financing, fixed asset purchased, project financing etc.
	Bay` Bithaman 'Ajil	This contract refers to the sale of goods on a deferred payment basis. Equipment or goods requested by the clients are bought by the bank which subsequently sells the goods to the client at an agreed price which includes the bank's markup (profit). The client may be allowed to settle the payment by instalments within a pre-agreed period, or in a lump sum. Similar to a murabahah contract, but with payment on a deferred basis.	This financing mode is suitable for working capital financing, fixed asset purchased, project financing etc.
	Bay` al-Salam	A contract of sale of goods where the price is paid in advance and the goods are delivered in the future.	This financing mode is suitable for agricultural financing which requires capital at certain critical stage (e.g. during plantation stage).
	Bay` al-Istisna'	A contract of acquisition of goods by specification or order, where the price is paid in advance, but the goods are manufactured and delivered at a later date.	This financing mode is suitable for financing assets which require capital at different stages of construction and tailor made manufacturing.
	Ijarah	A contract under which a bank purchases and leases out equipment required by its clients for a rental fee. The duration of the lease and rental fees are agreed in advance. Ownership of the equipment remains in the hands of the bank.	This instrument is suitable for financing fixed assets such as machinery, motor vehicles etc.
			Contd...

Contd...			
3. Voluntary charitable contract (tabarru)	Ar-Rahn	A pawning contract which involves holding a valuable non-fungible good as insurance against a debt, where the nonfungible may be used to extract the value of the debt or part thereof. In some jurisdiction, a minimum custodian fee may be charged to the borrower for safekeeping of pawned property.	This financing mode is suitable for all purposes including working capital, personal consumption, fixed assets purchase etc. This mode of financing requires customer to have valuable asset eligible for pawning such as gold or silver.
	Qard al-Hassan	An interest-free loan given mainly for welfare purposes. The borrower is only required to pay back the amount borrowed. In some cases, a minimum administrative fee may also be charged to the borrower. However, this service charge must be the actual administrative cost incurred in managing the loan and not a fixed percentage on the amount of loan.	This financing mode is suitable for all purposes including working capital, personal consumption, fixed assets purchase etc.
4. Hybrid	Musharakah Mutanaqisah	This instrument involves three different contracts, namely musharakah, sale and ijarah. Islamic banks jointly purchase and own an asset with client aiming at transferring the ownership to the client. The bank's share will gradually be redeemed by client by executing sales contract. The bank is also allowed to lease its portion of the asset to client for rental income.	This financing instrument is suitable for fixed asset financing.
	Ijarah Thumma al-bay	This instrument involves two separate contracts namely leasing and sales contracts executed separately and in sequence. The bank normally purchases the asset and leases it to client. At the end of leasing period, the ownership is transferred to the client by executing sales contract which normally at a nominal price.	This financing instrument is suitable for fixed asset financing such as motor vehicles.

5. Financing Through Special Purpose Vehicle (SPV)

A major concern for banks to be involved in microfinance is how to manage their risk inherent in financing activities involving the poor and small entrepreneurs. The issue of risk is paramount especially in banking business that requires efficient and effective mechanisms and instruments in managing asset and liability on banks' balance sheet to ensure their viability and sustainability.

One of the possible alternatives for banks to get involved in microfinance is through a special purpose vehicle or popularly known as SPV. An SPV is a legal entity created by a firm (known as the sponsor or originator) to undertake some specific purpose or restricted activity spelt out by the sponsoring firm (Gorton & Souleles, 2005). The SPV may be a subsidiary of the sponsoring firm or it may be an independent SPV, which is not consolidated with the sponsoring firm for tax, accounting or legal purposes. The latter has an added feature of being a bankruptcy remote entity.

The legal form for an SPV may be a limited partnership, a limited liability company, a trust, or a corporation (Gorton & Souleles, 2005). In case of Malaysia, SPV normally takes the legal form of a trust and governed by Trustee Act. SPV is a trust set up to fulfil specific purposes. In this regard, it can perform specific microfinance activities to benefit certain beneficiaries. The trustee will be appointed by the sponsoring bank to oversee the operations and activities outlined in the trust deed. More importantly, the designated funds channelled by the bank as a form of trust should be used only for the prescribed objectives.

An essential feature of an SPV which makes it promising as a vehicle to offer microfinance is its bankruptcy remote in nature. This implies that should the sponsoring firm or Islamic bank enter a bankruptcy procedure, the firm's creditors cannot seize the assets of the SPV. To ensure the SPV as bankruptcy remote as possible, its activities can be restricted. For instance, it can be restricted from issuing debt beyond a stated limit (Gorton & Souleles, 2005; Standard and Poor, 2002). The shares are customarily being held by a charitable trust established for that purpose. The trust will be the sole shareholder in the SPV. There must also be no provision in the constitutional documents of the SPV giving the sponsoring bank a right to control the affairs of the SPV. Standard and Poor (2002) provides the following list of characteristics for a bankruptcy remote SPV:

- Restrictions on objects, powers and purposes
- Limitations on ability to incur indebtedness
- Restrictions or prohibitions on merger, consolidation, dissolution, liquidation, winding up, asset sales, transfers of equity interests, and amendments to the organisational documents relating to "separateness"
- Incorporation of separateness covenants restricting dealings with parents and affiliates
- "Non-petition" language (i.e., a covenant not to file the SPV into involuntary bankruptcy)
- Security interests over assets
- An independent director (or functional equivalent) whose consent is required for the filing of a voluntary bankruptcy petition.

Based on the above discussion of SPV, this paper suggests that Islamic banks may establish an SPV by allocating certain amount of funds for microfinance purposes. The Articles of Association of the SPV will limit its business activities to a particular activity of the deal, such as the microfinance. The SPV must be fully bankruptcy-remote so that the Islamic bank is fully protected from the failure of the SPV and hence maintaining its viability and sustainability in banking business. This means, for instance, that it cannot be a subsidiary of the Islamic bank. The transfer of funds must be on a "full sale" basis for accountancy and regulatory purposes. There must not be any possibility of the SPV being consolidated with the selling bank. The benefits to the bank will be lost if the accounts of the SPV are consolidated with those of the selling bank.

The basic procedures of microfinance through SPV are straightforward and summarised in figure 3 below. The key elements are as follows:

- The Islamic bank mobilises various sources of funds with specific microfinance objectives
- The Islamic bank creates a bankruptcy-remote SPV
- The bank allocates certain amount of funds and pass it to the SPV

- The funds are channelled to various clients depending on needs and demands. For example, zakah funds may only be allocated to poor clients for consumption purposes and capacity building initiatives, while other type of funds can be used to finance their productive economic activities.

Figure 3: Financing Via SPV

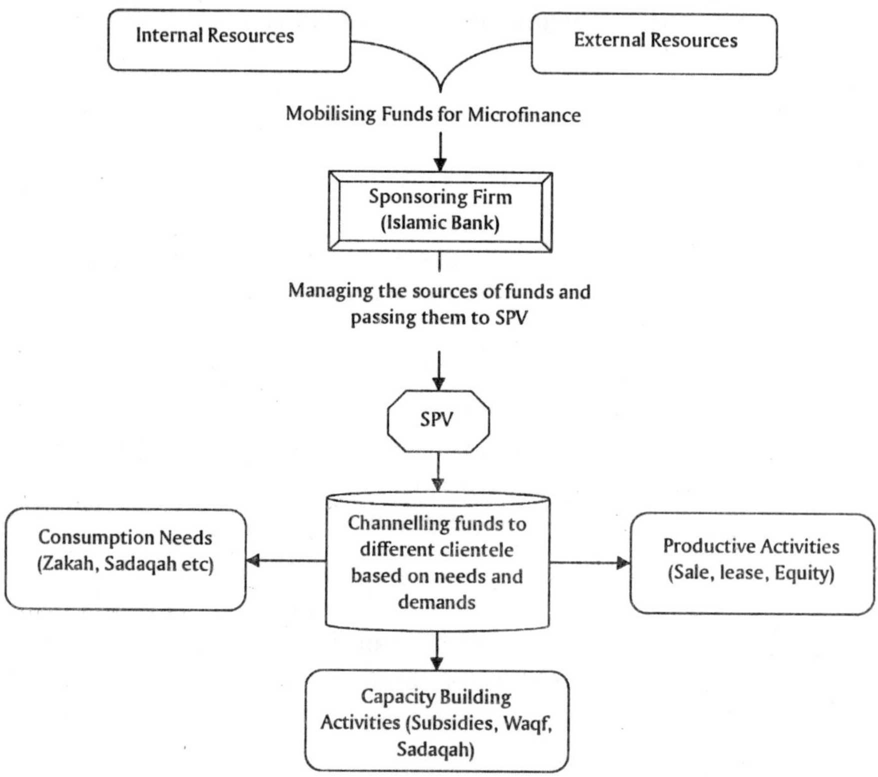

6. Conclusion

This paper highlights the relevance of microfinance as a globally accepted practice to Islamic banks. The Islamic banking system has an in-built dimension that promotes financing activities to the poor, as it resides within a financial trajectory underpinned by the forces of Shariah injunctions. These Shariah injunctions interweave Islamic financial transactions with genuine concern for poverty eradication, social justice and equal distribution of wealth at the same time as prohibiting involvement in illegal activities which are detrimental to social and environmental well-being.

Perhaps, after more than 30 years of impressive growth, it is time for the industry to be reoriented to emphasize on issues relating to social and economic ends of financial transactions, rather than overemphasizing on making profits and meeting the bottom line alone. There are fundamental differences between Islamic banking and conventional banking, not only in the ways they practise their business, but above all the values which guide Islamic banking whole operation and outlook. The values as prevailed within the ambit of Shariah are expressed not only in the minutiae of its transactions, but in the breadth of its role in society. This demands the internalisation of Shariah principles on Islamic financial transactions, in its form, spirit and substance. By so doing, it epitomises the objectives of Shariah in promoting economic and social justice.

As reviewed in this paper, microfinance requires innovative approaches beyond the traditional financial intermediary role. Among others, building human capacity through social intermediation and designing group-based lending programmes are proven to be among the effective tools to reduce transaction costs and lower exposure to numerous financial risks in relation to providing credit to the rural poor. Group based approach also foster a better flow of information between lenders and borrowers and hence less adverse selection and moral hazard in the credit market.

The success of various approaches used in microfinance programme worldwide should be emulated by Islamic banks. Additionally, Islamic banks may benefit from spectrum of sources of funds and offer a wide array of financing instruments catering different needs and demands of their clients. This paper also suggests the use of special purpose vehicle, SPV as one of the possible alternatives for channelling funds to the poor. With its unique bankruptcy-remote feature, Islamic banks are fully protected from any failure of SPV that involves microfinance activities. In the final analysis, Islamic banks can practise microfinance without compromising with institutional viability, competitiveness and sustainability.

(Asyraf Wajdi Dusuki, Department of Economics, Kulliyyah of Economics and Management Sciences, International Islamic University Malaysia, Kuala Lumpur, Malaysia. The author can be reached at asyraf.w@iiu.edu.my).

Endnotes

1 Transaction costs have a large fixed-cost component, so unit costs for smaller savings deposits or smaller loans are high compared with those for larger transactions. The conventional banks are structured to handle much larger individual transactions or loans than those required by the poor. Lending to the poor who normally demand small amount of loans is regarded expensive because of high overhead costs. See (Jacklen, 1988; Zeller & Meyer, 2002)

2 Grameen Bank (Bangladesh) which started operation in 1976 has now a daily loan volume of $1.5 million and has 98 percent repayment rate, appears to be a model of success in applying this mechanism. One of the distinctive characteristics to the Grameen Bank is that loans are made to self-formed groups of approximately five farmers, who are mutually responsible for repaying the loans. Additional amounts of loans will be further granted if all members of the group have settled all the outstanding amounts. In such arrangement, Stiglitz (1990) argued that the Grameen Bank devised an incentive structure called 'peer monitoring' whereby the others within the village do the monitoring on their behalf by exploiting the local knowledge of the members of the group. However, Besley and Coate (1995) and Hulme and Mosley (1996) assert that even though the group-lending may prove to have a positive effect on enhancing the incentive of loan repayment, it may have perverse effect when the whole group defaults, even when some members would have repaid individually.

3 Many of the transaction costs arise from the need to acquire information about the counter-parties involve in transaction. Obtaining such information for small loans can be costly if the bank agent is asked to do this. Traditional financial intermediation techniques, such as judging the loan application based on written information, are either not feasible due to the illiteracy or too costly to administer. However, information about the creditworthiness of a loan applicant is readily available within the local community through neighbours and peers, which can be obtained at least cost if networks or institutions are based at community level.

4 In their model, Besley and Coate (1995) postulate a social penalty function that describes the punishments available within a group rather than the bank. This social penalty implies that members in the community who do not comply with the norms, trust and values of the communities can be ridiculed or ousted from the family. This may constitute a powerful incentive device, since the costs of upsetting other members in the community may be high.

5 In Tanzania, social capital at the community level impacted poverty by making government services more effective, facilitating the spread of information on agriculture, enabling groups to pool their resources and manage property as a cooperative, and giving people access to

credit who have been traditionally locked out of formal financial institutions. For details, data analysis and empirical studies refer (Narayan & Pritchett, 1999)

6 In their paper, Hoff and Stiglitz (1998) demonstrate two ways that a subsidy may increase equilibrium prices in a monopolistically competitive market. There may be induced entry and a resulting loss of scale in economies, or induced entry with negative externalities in enforcement across suppliers. The paper explores these issues in a context where enforcement problems are particularly acute and expenditures on enforcement are often large especially in rural credit markets in developing countries. According to them, in a monopolistically competitive market where there is free entry into moneylending, a subsidy has been found to induce new entry, and eventually the new entry reduces the market of each moneylender. This forces him to operate at a higher marginal cost of transacting loans. Thus, it increases the marginal cost of lending. On the other hand, they also present alternative argument that the subsidies may cause the marginal cost of moneylenders to rise. In this model, an increase in entry adversely affects borrowers' incentives to repay, which increases the enforcement effort that each moneylender must expand per borrower to ensure repayment. New entry thereby raises each moneylender's cost of taking on an additional customer. See (Hoff & Stiglitz, 1998).

References

Adams, D. W., & Vogel, R. C. (1986). Rural financial markets in low-income countries: Recent contoversies and lessons. *World Development, 14*(4), 477-487.

Ahmad, K. (2000). Islamic Finance and Banking: The Challenge and Prospects. *Review of Islamic Economics, 9*, 57-82.

Ahmad, Z. (1984). *Concept and Models of Islamic Banking: An Assessment.* Paper presented at the Seminar on Islamisation of Banking, Karachi.

Akerlof, G. (1970). The Market of Lemons. *Quarterly Journal of Economics, 17*, 488-500.

Akhtar, M. R. (1996). Practice and Prospects of Musharaka Financing for Small Enterprises in Pakistan. *Journal of Islamic Banking and Finance, 13*(3), 7-27.

Akhtar, M. R. (1998). Islamic Microfinance: Credit Where Credit Is Really Due. *Islamic Banker, October*, 8-9.

Al-Harran, S. (1995). *Proposal For An Integrated Marketing Model of Musharakah Financing To Help Disadvantaged Fishing People in Malaysia.* Paper presented at the International workshop on Islamic Partnership Financing For Small Enterprise. Organised by the Enterprise Development Centre, Cranfield Scholl of Management of England, Cairo, Egypt.

Al-Harran, S. (1996). Islamic Finance Needs A New Paradigm. *New Horizon, 48* (February), 7-9.

Al-Harran, S. (1999). Islamic Partnership Financing. *Arab Law Quarterly, 14*(3), 193-202.

Al-Harran, S. A. S. (1990). *Islamic Finance: The Experience of The Sudanese Islamic Bank in Partnership (Musharakah) Financing As A Tool For Rural Development Among Small Farmers in Sudan.* Unpublished PhD Thesis, Durham University, Durham.

Al-Omar, F., & Abdel-Haq, M. (1996). *Islamic Banking: Theory, Practice and Challenges.* London & New Jersey: Zed Books.

Al-ZamZami, A., & Grace, L. (2000). *Islamic Banking Principles Applied to Microfinance: Case Study of Honeidah Microfinance Programmes, Yemen.* New York: United Nations Capital Development Fund (UNCDF).

Bennett, L., & Cuevas, C. E. (1996). Sustainable Banking With The Poor. *Journal of International Development, 8*(No.2), 145-152.

Bennett, L., Goldberg, M., & Hunte, P. (1996). Ownership and Sustainability: Lessons on Group-Based Financial Services From South Asia. *Journal of International Development, 8*(2), 271-288.

Besley, T., & Coate, S. (1995). Group Lending, repayment incentives and social collateral. *Journal of Development Economics, 46*, 1-18.

Bhatt, N., & Tang, S.-Y. (1998). The Problem of Transaction Costs in Group-Based Microlending: An Institutional Perspective. *World Development, 26*(4), 623-637.

Braverman, A., & Guasch, J. L. (1986). Rural Credit Markets and Institutions in Developing Countries: Lessons for Policy Analysis from Practice and Modern Theory. *World Development, 14*(10/11), 1253-1267.

Chapra, M. U. (1987). *Towards an Islamic Financial System.* Paper presented at the International Seminar on Islamic Economics, International Islamic University Malaysia, Kuala Lumpur.

Chapra, M. U. (2000b). Why has Islam Prohibited Interest: Rationale behind the Prohibition of Interest. *Review of Islamic Economics, 9*, 5-20.

Collier, P. (1998). *Social Capital and Poverty.* Washinton D.C.: World Bank.

Daripa, A. (2000). *Market for "Right-to-Borrow": A Theory of Credit Cooperatives. Discussion Papers in Economics.* London: Department of Economics, University of London.

Dhumale, R., & Sapcanin, A. (1998). *An Application of Islamic Banking Principles to Microfinance.* New York: Regional Bureau for Arab States, United Nations Development Programme.

Diamond, D. (1991). Monitoring and Reputation: The Choice Between Bank Loans and Directly Placed Debt. *Journal of Political Economy, 99*, 689-721.

Gorton, G., & Souleles, N. S. (2005). Special Purpose Vehicles and Securitization, *NBER Working Paper No.11190*: National Bureau of Economic Research.

Gurgad, M., Pederson, G., & Yaron, J. (1994). *Outreach and sustainability of six rural finance institutions in Sub-Saharan Africa*. Washinton D.C.: The World Bank.

Hassan, M. K., & Alamgir, D. A. H. (2002). Microfinancial Services and Poverty Alleviation in Bangladesh: A Comparative Analysis of Secular and Islamic NGOs. In M. Iqbal (Ed.), *Islamic Economic Institutions and the Elimination of Poverty*. Leicestershire: The Islamic Foundation.

Hoff, K., & Stiglitz, J. E. (1998). Moneylenders and bankers: price-increasing subsidies in a monopolistically competitive market. *Journal of Development Economics, 55*, 485-518.

Holmstrom, B., & Tirole, J. (1993). *Financial Intermediation, loanable funds, and the real sector*: IDEI Toulouse University.

Hulme, D., & Mosley, P. (1996). *Finance Against Poverty* (First ed. Vol. 1). London: Routledge.

Ibn Ashur. (2006). *Treatise on Maqasid al-Shari'ah* (M. E.-T. El-Mesawi, Trans.). London: The International Institute of Islamic Thought.

Iqbal, M., & Molyneux, P. (2005). *Thirty Years of Islamic Banking: History, Performance and Prospects*. New York: Palgrave Macmillan.

Jacklen, H. R. (1988, 1989). *Banking on the Informal Sector*. Paper presented at the International Conference on Microenterprise Development, Washinton, USA.

Khan, M. S., & Mirakhor, A. (1987). The Framework and Practice of Islamic Banking. In M. S. Khan & A. Mirakhor (Eds.), *Theoretical Studies in Islamic Banking and Finance*. Texas, USA: The Institute for Research and Islamic Studies.

Krishna, A., Uphoff, N., & Esman, M. J. (1997). *Reasons for Hope: Instructive Experiences in Rural Development*. West Hartford: Kumanrian Press.

Ledgerwood, J. (1999). *Microfinance Handbook: An Institutional and Financial Perspective (Sustainable Banking with the Poor)*. Washinton: The World Bank.

Littlefield, E., Morduch, J., & Hashemi, S. (2003). *Is Microfinance an Effective Strategy to Reach the Millennium Develoment Goals?* Washinton D.C.: CGAP.

Metwally, M. M. (1997). Economic Consequences of Applying Islamic Principles in Muslim Societies. *International Journal of Social Economics, 24*(7/8/9), 941-957.

Narayan, D., & Pritchett, L. (1999). Cents and Sociability: Households Income and Social Capital in Rural Tanzania. *Economic Development and Cultural Change, 47*(4), 871-897.

Otero, M., & Rhyne, E. H. (1994). *The New World of Microenterprise Finance. Building Healthy Financial Institutions For the Poor.* West Hartford, CN: Kumarian Press Inc.

Pischke, J. D. V. (1991). *Finance at the Frontier. Debt Capacity and the Role of Credit in the Private Economy. EDI Development Studies.* Washinton D.C.: World Bank, Economic Development Institute (EDI).

Pischke, J. D. V. (1996). Measuring the Trade-off Between Outreach and Sustainability of Microenterprise Lenders. *Journal of International Development, 8* (Number 2), 225-239.

Pischke, J. D. V., Adams, D. W., & Donald, G. (1986). *Rural Financial Markets in Developing Countries.* Washinton D.C.: The Economic Development Institute of The World Bank.

Pitt, M. M., & Khandker, S. R. (1996). *Household and intrahousehold impact of the Grameen Bank and similar targeted credit programs in Bangladesh.* Unpublished manuscript, Washinton D.C.

Rhyne, E., & Otero, M. (1992). Financial services for Microenterprises: Principles and Institutions. *World Development, 20*(11), 1561-1571.

Rhyne, E., & Otero, M. (1994). Financial services for microentrepreneurs: principles and institutions. In M. Otero & E. Rhyne (Eds.), *The New World of Microenterprise Finance: Building Healthy Financial Institutions for the Poor.* West Hartford: Kumarian Press.

Robinson, M. S. (2001). *The Microfinance Revolution: Sustainable Finance For The Poor* (1st ed.). Washinton: The World Bank.

Rosly, S. A., & Bakar, M. A. A. (2003). Performance of Islamic and Mainstream Banks in Malaysia. *International Journal of Social Economics, 30*(12), 1249-1265.

Seibel, H. D., & Parhusip, U. (1998, October 1998). Rural Bank Shinta Daya:Attaining Outreach with Sustainability – A Case Study of a Private Microfinance Institution in Indonesia. *IDS Bulletin, 29.*

Siddiqi, M. N. (1983). *Issues in Islamic Banking.* Leicester, United Kingdom: The Islamic Foundation.

Siddiqi, M. N. (1985). *Partnership and Profit-Sharing in Islamic Law.* Leicester, U.K.: The Islamic Foundation.

Siddiqui, S. H. (2001). Islamic Banking: True Modes of Financing. *New Horizon, 109* (May-June).

Sinclair, P. J. N. (1998). *Why do the Poor Save so Little?* (Department of Economics Discussion Paper). Birmingham: Department of Economics Discussion Paper, University of Birmingham.

Standard and Poor. (2002). *U.S. Legal Criteria for "Recycled" Special Purpose Entities.*Unpublished manuscript.

Stiglitz, J. E. (1990). Peer Monitoring and Credit Markets. *The World Bank Economic Review, 4*(3), 351-366.

Vogel, R. C. (1984). Savings Mobilization: The Forgotten Half of Rural Finance. In D. W.Adams, G. D.H & J. D. V. Pischke (Eds.), *Undermining Rural Development with Cheap Credit* (pp. 248-265): Westview Press.

Zeller, M., & Meyer, R. L. (2002). Improving the Performance of Microfinance: Financial Sustainability, Outreach and Impact. In M. Zeller & R. L. Meyer (Eds.), *The Triangle of Microfinance: Financial Sustainability, Outreach and Impact.* Baltimore: The John Hopkins University Press.

Zeller, M., & Sharma, M. (1998). *Rural Finance and Poverty Alleviation. Food Policy Report.* Washinton D.C.: International Food Policy Research Institute.

6

Ethical Money: Financial Growth in the Muslim World

Bjorn Sorenson

Current financial crises, such as the bursting of the housing bubble in the United States and the accompanying credit crunch, highlight the need for greater moral inquiry into the structure of financial regulation. The development of Socially Responsible Investing and the proliferation of Shariah-compliant finance bring much-needed ethical scrutiny to financial investments. As the Islamic financial services industry develops, it faces obstacles in creating new Shariah products, developing common practices to approve such products, and in serving niche and retail consumers. New legal customs and new legal scholarship provide lawyers a unique opportunity for the development of transnational business practices, the examination of the ethics of finance, and the chance to participate in substantive dialogue about morality in a globalizing world.

Source: American University International Law Review, Vol.23, No.4, 2008

Introduction

Money is a moral issue, and ethical considerations pervade the Islamic financial services industry through *Shariah* law. Islamic finance and finance in the Muslim world is growing quickly, and conventional financial institutions will continue to accommodate demand for *Shariah*-compliant banking and investment services.[1] As the field of Islamic finance grows and globalizes, the relation between *Shariah*-compliant financial products and conventional financial products deserves more consideration as an area of law on the international stage. At the nexus of legal, financial, and religious issues, scholarly research in this area is ripe for development and presents an opportunity for cultural dialogue.

This introductory comment provides a brief overview of important issues in the financial growth of the Muslim world. This Issue of the *American University International Law Review* includes three pieces that contribute to understanding this growth. Ali Adnan Ibrahim addresses the growth of customary practices in Islamic Finance.[2] Umar F. Moghul provides an example of the complex structure involved when structuring a leveraged buyout transaction in accordance with *Shariah* principles.[3] Finally, Dr. Bashar H. Malkawi and Dr. Haitham A. Haloush provide a thorough overview of the new Securities Law of Jordan.[4]

I. Morality, Challenges, and Dialogue in Islamic Finance

A. Finance and Morality

Most discussions of Islamic finance focus on certain prohibitions, "contract mechanics, and certification of Islamicity by 'Shari'a Supervisory Boards.'"[5] However, to fully understand Islamic finance, scholars and practitioners need to make an explicit connection between the morals that underpin *Shariah* and the structure that the law imposes. Ali Adnan Ibrahim provides an excellent introduction to the moral underpinnings of *Shariah* finance in his article, "The Rise of Customary Businesses in International Financial Markets."[6] According to Ibrahim, Islamic finance goes well beyond a common understanding of the prohibition of usury and excessive risk, to embrace ethical and religious goals, including a quest for justice.[7] Further, Islamic finance embraces the philosophy of "risk sharing and the promotion of social and economic welfare" which extends "beyond profit maximization."[8] These values often come into direct conflict with products and practices of the prevailing capitalist economy. The current financial crises affecting the US economy and the growth of "social screening" highlight how moral issues pervade the current economy.

The current financial crisis in the United States is also a moral crisis. Thousands of homeowners face foreclosure. The Federal Open Markets Committee balances the need to cut interest rates and bail out failing institutions such as Bear Stearns without succumbing to "moral hazard."[9] This financial conundrum raises the following questions: Should regulations allow homeowners to enter into mortgages that they cannot afford to pay? Should the government assist homeowners who face foreclosure? Does bailing out ailing derivatives dealers create an incentive for further risky behavior in the future? If Bear Stearns falls, is it *just* to allow other institutions to collapse and send a severe disruption through the global economy?[10]

Islamic finance is based on an understanding of economic justice.[11] Prohibitions against *riba*, or interest, must be considered in a moral framework.[12] Additionally, Islam prohibits excessive *gharar* (uncertainty) and *maisir* (gambling).[13] *Maisir*, for example, may divert attention and resources from a productive occupation,[14] and earning a profit directly as a result of another's loss is immoral.[15] Even conventional debt is seen as "a recipe for exploitation."[16]

Rippling through the global economy is a reminder of interconnectedness. Much of the current financial crisis is based on the entanglement of parties in derivatives and the uncertain value of these instruments. Investor Warren Buffett said of derivatives, "Like Hell, (they) are easy to enter and almost impossible to exit."[17] As a moral issue, therefore, "(t)here is a need to focus on the social relationships that monetary transaction involves, not the objects that mediate those relationships."[18] Though Islamic financial instruments do not allow for the spectacular gains and collapses that regularly churn through the capitalist economy, they do excel morally by integrating ethics into the financial system. Where capitalism rewards a risk-taking individual, Islamic finance explicitly limits risk for the betterment of society as a whole.

Despite elaborate equations such as the Black-Scholes model and other instruments that analysts and accountants use to try to quantify risk, *gharar* and *maisir* pervade derivative financial instruments. At any given time, there is no reliable way to determine the value of a derivative asset,[19] and no real approximation of how far negative effects may spread in the market. Buffett summarizes the *gharar* and *maisir* of derivatives colorfully and aptly: "(D)erivatives are financial weapons of mass destruction, carrying dangers that, while now latent, are potentially lethal."[20]

The second issue highlighting morality in the global economy is the growth of ethically screened products. Islamic financial products, which prohibit involvement with alcohol, tobacco, and gambling, for example, screen for ethical issues in accordance with *Shariah*.[21] According to one analyst, "The issue of whether ethical investment will become coupled with Islamic finance and become a major theme in global financial markets is one of the big new developments in the growth of Islamic finance."[22] These ethical screens are similar to growing practices in Socially Responsible Investing ("SRI"). SRI examines potential investments for "environmental, social, and governance issues," and parallels *Shariah* objectives "in terms of welfare and well-being."[23] "As an economic system based on values other than pure monetary gain," Michael Gassner notes, "Islamic finance tends to parallel its natural benchmark . . . SRI."[24]

Connecting the financial crisis with ethical implications of SRI and *Shariah* investment, Michael Gassner also urges institutions to "consider[] the social impact of housing price bubbles, the mess in the back office of credit derivative swaps, the asset/liability mismatches of hedge funds and the unsustainable debt policies of even highly developed countries."[25] One prominent SRI provider, the Calvert Group, attracts investors who seek to "align their investment portfolio with their personal values," "encourage(s) improved corporate social and environmental performance through active investment strategy," and "identif[(ies) companies with better long-term financial performance through the analysis of social and environmental factors."[26] Although not a fund provider itself, Dow Jones has created the Dow Jones Islamic Market Indexes to track *Shariah*-compliant portfolios.[27] These indexes are maintained under strict screening criteria in accordance with *Shariah* law, and monitored by an independent *Shariah* Supervisory Board.[28]

B. Challenges to the Growth of Islamic Finance

Although the Islamic financial services industry as a whole is growing at record pace, two factors inhibit accelerated expansion. First, the creation of *Shariah*-compliant financial products is a time-consuming process because of the unique structures and rigorous approval process. Secondly, it remains difficult to get *Shariah*-compliant financial products and services to ordinary consumers around the globe.

1. Creation of *Shariah* Products

According to the Report of the Islamic Capital Market Task Force of the International Organization of Securities Commissions, Islamic financial institutions build modern financial products in two ways: by modifying conventional products and services to comply with *Shariah* principles, and by applying *Shariah* principles to develop new products and services.[29] This first mechanism, often called "*Shariah* arbitrage," uses established financial products as a model and then modifies aspects or structure to achieve the same effect while remaining in compliance with *Shariah* law.[30] However, some creative arbitrage strategies are considered *hiyal*, or "artifice," and are frowned upon by *Shariah* boards.[31]

Ibrahim's survey of various forms of financial engineering includes many traditional and contemporary contract forms, as well as an overview of Islamic banking, hedge funds, investment banking, hedging and derivatives, and real estate investment trusts.[32] Moghul provides a specific example of innovation in Islamic acquisition financing structure. A leveraged buyout, typically reliant on massive amounts of debt, was engineered to comply with *Shariah* principles via a unique sale-leaseback structure involving two tranches of financing. Moghul describes the difficulty of implementing such a complex transaction using *Shariah* principles.[33]

After a product is created, it must be submitted to an independent *Shariah* Advisory Board for approval. However, many religious scholars face an ethical dilemma by acting as both independent auditor and inside consultant.[34] Very often the product is structured in consultation with the *Shariah* Advisory Board. For example, Ibrahim notes that, "The ensuing economic pressure on jurisconsults has resulted in a widespread practice of circumventing tactics by relying upon obscurely minority views in order to push through the contemplated transactional structure."[35] Similarly, in his review of the *Shariah*-compliant leveraged buyout transaction, Moghul notes that the *Shariah* board in the transaction worked closely with counsel and the banks to structure many aspects of the deal.

Apart from individual approval of custom-made deals, many Islamic financial institutions follow the Accounting and Auditing Organization for Islamic Financial Institutions ("AAOIFI") Standards.[36] These standards allow financial organizations to comply with *Shariah* standards, and also create confidence in the consumer market.[37]

While the regulation of many conventional financial products and industries are rule-based, the AAOIFI standards are principles-based.[38]

For example, in their discussion of the Securities Law of Jordan, Malkawi and Haloush note that Jordanian regulations "follow the philosophy that the government does not guarantee the quality of investments, but rather assures that all the information is disclosed to the investing public."[39] In addition, the Jordanian Securities Commission has flexible control of market regulation by promulgating principle-based directives rather than laws.[40] As Christine Walsh recently noted in her article contrasting the spirit of rule-based Sarbanes-Oxley regulations with the principles inherent in *Shariah* finance, there is a tension between AAOIFI guiding principles and "American corporate law . . . based on the enforcement of rules."[41] In addition to rules-principles tension, a tension remains between merit-based review of financial products and open disclosure regulation, where the consumer is left to make investment choices based on the information available.

The entire debate, however, is not reducible to rules versus principles. The AAOIFI produces standards, but each institution may have its own *Shariah* Advisory Board to approve financial services. Each board may make different interpretations of *Shariah* compliance based on different schools of thought in Islamic jurisprudence.[42] Ibrahim describes the development of different interpretive schools over time and notes, "The total number of the Traditions in the two most authentic compilations of the Sunni school is about 10,000, which includes a significant number of Traditions that relate to trade, business and other financial transactions."[43]

Because there is currently no universal consensus of *Shariah* interpretation, "different jurisdictions have adopted different practices in relation to various Islamic capital market products and services."[44] It is unlikely that a universal consensus of juristic opinion will form. Although some scholars, Ibrahim explains, favor a consensus of a *majority* of jurists to be binding, "the popular view favors the consensus of *all* jurists."[45] The lack of "best practices for regulation concerning significant areas such as *Shariah* certification, the establishment of *Shariah* boards, qualifications of *Shariah* advisors and enhanced disclosure relating to Islamic capital market products"[46] could inhibit the development and expansion of uniform Islamic financial services by limiting cross-border flows and could encourage fractionalization among interpretation and region.[47] Ibrahim's article provides a valuable starting point to consider these growing customary practices.

2. Reaching Consumers

The increased scrutiny of Islamic charities and financial institutions by US regulators and investigative authorities after September 11, 2001 has encouraged many to pull assets from the United States.[48] Wealthy Muslims, institutions, and consumers looking "for products and modes of investment that are acceptable and in compliance with . . . *Shariah*"[49] "have been the catalyst towards making the Islamic financial services industry a flourishing industry."[50] Now there are 550 Islamic financial institutions located in more than 75 countries.[51] This growth is not just in traditionally Islamic countries, but in areas such as Europe and the United States as well, reflecting the global reach of Islamic values.[52] Even conventional banks, such as ABNAmro, Chase, Citi, and others have developed Islamic banking units.[53]

As mentioned, financial institutions that openly comply with AAOIFI standards attract consumers who seek confidence that their investments are *Shariah* compliant. However, the Islamic Capital Market Fact Finding Report notes that educating investors "with regards to Islamic capital market products . . . is critical to improving investor activism as well as enhancing investor protection and scrutiny of Islamic capital market activities. Discerning investors typically demand higher standards of service, and this in turn would contribute to the development of higher standards being applied by market practitioners."[54] Convergence of interpretations and harmonization of *Shariah* principles could increase demand and accelerate growth of Islamic financial services and products.[55]

One example of accelerated growth in the Muslim world is reflected in the Jordanian Securities Law of 2002. Malkawi and Haloush note that, unlike regulation of established markets such as those in the United States and the United Kingdom, "Jordanian regulation is designed to assist in building and developing the market."[56] Jordan liberalized and deregulated its commercial banking sector in the early 1990s with great success and increased efficiency.[57] Now Jordan seeks to encourage broader participation in the securities markets, while at the same time educating participants on the market. According to the authors, Jordanians, "unfamiliar with the workings of the securities market, must gain an understanding of the process (of investing in a securities market) and begin to develop a sense of true risk/reward decisions."[58] Islamic finance needs to "reach out to the poor, defining them as customers with profitable needs rather than as an indigent and commercially nonexistent market segment."[59] In addition to seeking out the poor and "unbanked" classes, financial institutions would do well to create services accessible to women, such as "ladies' banks" in the United Arab Emirates.[60] As this growth trend continues, Islamic financial services and products will transition from an investment niche to a "core offering for conventional financial institutions."[61]

C. Dialogue in International Law

As noted by Moghul, much of the development of new *Shariah*-compliant financial products is done with the patient and flexible assistance of legal counsel.[62] Similarly, Ibrahim notes that much recent scholarship of Islamic finance has been through the reporting of deals by practitioners.[63] Since much of Islamic finance is tied to the legal field, it places lawyers in the somewhat unusual position of cultural intermediaries for dialogue.

Also, as Robert Bianchi points out, "as Islamic financial institutions develop in strength and scope, they interact more frequently with governments, conventional financial structures, multinational enterprises, and international organizations."[64] The integration of Islamic organizations with such so-called "Slaughter networks" strengthens the standing of *Shariah* financial ethics and the efficacy of their enforcement.[65] Ibrahim explains the steps taken by various Muslim countries—like Malaysia, Pakistan, and the United Arab Emirates—to standardize the regulation of the Islamic financial services industry within their countries.[66] However, the development of these regulatory bodies has extended beyond national borders. Islamic Development Bank practices are often followed as industry standards,[67] and other industry bodies such as the AAOIFI, the Islamic Financial Services Board, the International Islamic Financial Market, the Liquidity Management Center, and the International Islamic Rating Agency also contribute to the development of customary practices.[68] As discussed above, the development of customary practices for regulation of *Shariah* certification, *Shariah* advisory boards, and the qualification of *Shariah* advisors would be beneficial to the advancement of Islamic finance. The development of such standards and best practices will inevitably entail intra-religious dialogue as Islamic jurists debate the proper application of *Shariah* to financial products.

The growth of the Islamic financial services industry also presents an opportunity for dialogue about globalization, money, and values. As Islamic finance begins to reach a broader consumer class, resistance will undoubtedly arise in some corners of the Islamic world. For some, the entire concept of *Shariah* arbitrage presupposes the value of the capitalist endeavor, and engagement in such terms may be "tantamount to capitulation."[69] The philosophy of Islamic economics developed by Sayyid Qutb and Ali Shari'ati, for example, was a critique of capitalism and capitalist values.[70] Current radical ideology, such as that of Al-Qaida, draws on this early economic critique of capitalism to justify terrorist activities.[71] According to Ibrahim, Islamic finance and economics are not merely by-products of *Shariah* law, but central to Muslims' political identity.[72]

While this critique poses problems for the integration of *Shariah* finance into conventional financial institutions, it also presents an opportunity for transnational and inter-religious dialogue on the nature of money, values, and the structure of the global economy. As financial ethicist Catherine Cowley notes, "Above all (money takes away) the freedom not to be forced to evaluate everything by its monetary value, its market price; because where all values are reduced to market values, justice itself is reduced to a market concept."[73] Continued integration between conventional and Islamic financial services provides an opportunity to explore how notions of justice relate to finance and how globalizing financial institutions can help make the world a more ethical place.

Conclusion

Through their articles, Ibrahim, Moghul, Malkawi and Haloush contribute to the growing scholarship of Islamic finance. Current financial crises, such as the bursting of the housing bubble in the United States and the accompanying credit crunch, highlight the need for greater moral inquiry into the structure of financial regulation. The development of Socially Responsible Investing and the proliferation of *Shariah*-compliant finance bring much-needed ethical scrutiny to financial investments. As the Islamic financial services industry develops, it faces obstacles in creating new *Shariah* products, developing common practices to approve such products, and in serving niche and retail consumers. New legal customs and new legal scholarship provide lawyers a unique opportunity for the development of transnational business practices, the examination of the ethics of finance, and the chance to participate in substantive dialogue about morality in a globalizing world.

(Bjorn Sorenson is a JD candidate at the Washington College of Law and Articles Editor on the American University International Law Review. He completed a B.A. from Western Michigan University in music and comparative religion and a Master of Theological Studies from Harvard Divinity School. After graduation, he plans to join the New York office of Skadden, Arps, Slate, Meagher & Flom. He can be reached at bjorn_sorenson@post.harvard.edu).

Endnotes

1 Julian Walker, Islamic Growth Means Challenges 1-2 (2005), *available at www.shariahcap.com/news/images/Arab%20Financial%20Forum%20Islamic%20Growth%20Means%20Challenges%20Nov05.doc*

2 Ali Adnan Ibrahim, *The Rise of Customary Business in International* Financial Markets: An Introduction to Islamic Finance and the Challenges of *International Integration*, 23 AM. U. INT'L L. REV. 661 (2008).

3 Umar F. Moghul, *Separating the Good from the Bad: Developments in Islamic Acquisition Financing*, 23 AM. U. INT'L L. REV. 733 (2008).

4 Bashar H. Malkawi & Haitham A. Haloush, *Reflections on the Securities Law of Jordan*, 23 AM. U. INT'L L. REV. 763 (2008).

5 Mahmoud a. El-gamal, Islamic Finance: law, economics, and Practice 1 (2006).

6 Ibrahim, *supra* note 2.

7 Id. at 664.

8 Id.

9 Ethan Penner, *Our Financial Bailout Culture*, WALL ST. J., Apr. 11, 2008, at A17.

10 The Fed faced a similar dilemma in 2002 after the collapse of Long Term Capital Management. Warren Buffett noted, "The Fed acted because its leaders were fearful of what might have happened to other financial institutions had the LTCM domino toppled." Annual Letter from Warren Buffett to the Shareholders of Berkshire Hathaway Inc. (Feb. 21, 2003), available at *http://www.berkshirehathaway.com/letters/2002pdf.pdf* (hereinafter Buffett Letter).

11 Timur Kuran, Islam and Mammon: the economic predicaments of Islamism 103-20 (2004).

12 *See* M. Umer Chapra, *Why Has Islam Prohibited Interest? in* Interest in Islamic economics: understanding Riba 96-111 (Abdulkader Thomas ed., 2006) (discussing the relation between the prohibition of *riba* in Islamic financial transactions with the concept of ustice in *Shariah* law).

13 Report of the islamic capital market task force of the International organization of securities commissions, islamic capital Market fact finding report 7-8 (2004), available at *http://www.iosco.org/library/pubdocs/pdf/Ioscopd170.pdf* (hereinafter IOSCO Report).

14 Id. at 8.

15 Id.

16 Muhammad Ayub, Understanding Islamic Finance 4 (2007).

17 Buffett Letter, *supra* note 100, at 13.

18 Catherine Cowley, *Money, Finance and Morality in a Global Economy* 3 (Heythrop Institute for Religion Ethics and Public Life, Working Paper No. 2, 2005), available at *http://www.heythrop.ac.uk/images/stories/hirepl/publications/hirepl/working_paper2.pdf.*

19 In his critique of derivative instruments, Buffett notes, "In extreme cases, mark-to-model denigrates into what I would call mark-to-myth." Buffett Letter, *supra* note 10, at 13.

20 Id. at 15.

21 IOSCO Report, *supra* note 13, at 66.

22 Walker, *supra* note 1, at 3-4.

23 Michael Saleh Gassner, *Bringing Morality to Material Motives*, Business Islamica, at 23, Apr. 2007, available at *http://www.islamicfinance.de/opinion_sri.pdf.*

24 Id. at 22.

25 Id. at 23.

26 Calvert Group, An Introduction to Socially Responsible Investing, *http://www.calvertgroup.com/sri.html* (last visited May 9, 2008).

27 *See generally* Dow Jones Islamic Market Indexes, *http://www .djindexes.com/mdsidx/?event=showIslamic (last visited May 9, 2008). See* Dow Jones Indexes, Guide To The Dow Jones Islamic Market Indexes (2008), available at *http://www.djindexes.com/mdsidx/downloads/imi_rulebook.pdf* (listing screening criteria such as alcohol, tobacco, pork products, conventional financial services, weapons and defense, and entertainment, including hotels, casinos/gambling, cinema, pornography, etc.).

28 *See* M.H. Khatkhatay & Shariq Nisar, *Investment in Stocks: A Critical Review of Dow Jones* Shari'ah *Screening Norms*, available at *http://www. djindexes.com/mdsidx/downloads/Islamic/articles/DowJonesShariahScreeningNor ms.pdf.*

29 IOSCO Report, *supra* note 13, at 5.

30 *See generally* Mahmoud A. El-Gamal, *Limits and Dangers of* Shari'a *Arbitrage, in* Islamic Finance: Current Legal And Regulatory Issues 115 (S. Nazim Ali ed., 2005).

31 *See, e.g.*, Abrurrahman Habil, *The Tension Between Legal Values and Formalism in Contemporary Islamic Finance, in* Integrating Islamic Finance Into The Mainstream: Regulation, Standardization And Transparency 109-118 (S. Nazim Ali ed., 2007).

32 *See* Ibrahim, *supra* note 2, at 703-21.

33 *See generally* Moghul, *supra* note 3.

34 Robert R. Bianchi, *Islamic Finance and the International System: Integration Without Colonialism, in* Integrating Islamic Finance Into The Mainstream: Regulation, Standardization And Transparency, *supra* note 31, at 133, 136.

35 Ibrahim, *supra* note 2, at 687.

36 *See generally* AAOIFI-Accounting and Auditing Organization for Islamic Financial Institutions, *http://www.aaoifi.com* (last visited May 8, 2008).

37 Christine Walsh, *Ethics: Inherent in Islamic Finance Through* Shari'a *Law; Resisted in American Business Despite Sarbanes-Oxley*, 12 Fordham J. Corp. & fin. L. 753, 761 (2007).

38 Id. at 776.

39 Malkawi & Haloush, *supra* note 4, at 779.

40 *Id.* at 13-14.

41 Walsh, *supra* note 37, at 776.

42 IOSCO Report, *supra* note 13, at 65.

43 Ibrahim, *supra* note 2, at 679.

44 IOSCO Report, *supra* note 133, at 65.

45 Ibrahim, *supra* note 2, at 680.

46 IOSCO Report, *supra* note 13, at 72-73.

47 *Id.* at 65.

48 Ibrahim Warde, *Introduction* to *Integrating Islamic Finance into the Mainstream: Regulation, Standardization and Transparency*, *supra* note 31, at 3.

49 WALKER, *supra* note 1, at 2.

50 IOSCO Report, *supra* note 13, at 1.

51 Ayub, *supra* note 16, at 15.

52 Kilian Bälz, *Islamic Retail Finance in Europe: Market Potential and Legal Challenges, in Integrating Islamic Finance Into The Mainstream: Regulation, Standardization and Transparency*, *supra* note 31, at 119-132.

53 Barbara L. Seniawski, Riba *Today: Social Equity, the Economy, and Doing Business Under Islamic Law*, 39 Colum. J. Transnat'l l. 701, 720 (2001).

54 IOSCO Report, *supra* note 13, at 69-70.

55 Id. at 65.

56 Malkawi & Haloush, *supra* note 4, at 768.

57 Aktham Maghyereh, *The Effect of Financial Liberalization on the Efficiency of Financial Institutions: The Case of Jordanian Commercial Banks*, *in* Islam And Business: Cross-Cultural And Cross-National Perspectives 71-106 (Kip Becker ed., 2004).

58 Malkawi & Haloush, *supra* note 4, at 805.

59 Gassner, *supra* note 23, at 23.

60 *Gender Gulf*, The Economist, Apr. 12, 2008, at 86 (explaining that because women have had the ability to inherit property for centuries under Islamic law, yet have been underserved by the banking sector, women are therefore "sitting on fortunes of cash, land, and even jewellery").

61 Walker, *supra* note 1, at 2.

62 *See generally* Moghul, *supra* note 3.

63 Ibrahim, *supra* note 2, at 722.

64 Bianchi, *supra* note 34, at 133.

65 *See, e.g.*, Anne-Marie Slaughter, *Global Government Networks, Global Information Agencies, and Disaggregated Democracy*, 24Mich. J. Int. L. 1041 (2003); *see* Bianchi, *supra* note 34, at 133 (exploring "the possibilities of integrating Islamic finance into a more open network of multicultural structures capable of promoting global growth and equity, highlighting what international lawyers and international relations theorists have described as the emergence of 'international regimes' and 'transnational civil society'").

66 Ibrahim, *supra* note 2, at 669.

67 Id.

68 Id. at 669-70.

69 Charles Tripp, Islam And The Moral Economy: The Challenge Of Capitalism 150 (2006).

70 *See generally id.* at 150-193 (examining the "Repertoires of resistance: Islamic anti-capitalism").

71 *See* Paul Berman, *The Philosopher of Islamic Terror*, N.Y. Times mag., Mar. 23, 2003, at 24 (narrating the history of how Qutb's critique of the West grew into the present day *Al-Qaida* movement).

72 Ibrahim, *supra* note 2, at 665-67.

73 Cowley, *supra* note 18, at 13.

Section II

Country/Regional Experiences

7

Sri Lanka and the Scope for Islamic Banking

Faizal Salieh

Sri Lanka is one of the few non-Islamic countries to have legislated for Islamic banking. The revised Banking Act No 30 of 1988, as amended in 2005, allows both commercial banks and specialized banks to operate on a Shariah compliant basis. The regulators are becoming alive to the growing Islamic market segment, both local and global, and the global developments and trends in Islamic banking. Islamic bankers and Shariah scholars are scarce resources and are critical success factors to the industry's future growth and development.

Introduction

Sri Lanka is one of the few non-Islamic countries to have legislated for Islamic banking. The revised Banking Act No 30 of 1988, as amended in 2005, allows both commercial banks and specialized banks to operate on a Shariah compliant basis, including: "the acceptance of a sum of money in any manner or form from any person for a fixed period of time for investment in a business venture of the bank on the basis that

Source: www.IslamicFinanceNews.com © Islamic Finance News Guide 2006, January 2006 and Mr. Faizal Salieh, Amana Investments. Reprinted with permission.

profits or losses of the venture will be shared with the person from whom such money is accepted in a manner determined at the time the money is accepted." This landmark legislation came in after years of intensive discussions and lobbying by Amana Investments, the pioneer Islamic services provider in the country, with the Central Bank of Sri Lanka.

Political Environment

Sri Lanka is a democratic socialist republic which gained independence in 1948 from colonial powers. The President is the head of state, wielding executive powers based on the French model, and is elected for a term of six years. The national legislature is the parliament, with 225 members elected for five years. Local government is devolved to nine provincial councils elected once every four years.

The newly elected President, Mahinda Rajapakse, is keen to resolve the country's ethnic Tamil problem which has prevented the economy from reaching its full potential. The Cease Fire Agreement with the Liberation Tigers of Tamil Elam (LTTE) is still operational. The present regime's "pro-business and pro-poor" approach, which was strongly emphasized in its budget for 2006, is comparable to that of India. In his inaugural policy statement Mr Rajapakse indicated the need for an active private-public partnership process to rebuild a new Sri Lanka.

Demography

The majority of the country's 19.5 million population is Buddhist (77%), while Muslims constitute about 8.5%. Population growth in 2004 was around 1.1%.

The workforce is estimated to be about 8 million with labour participation (working population) of around 48% and unemployment at 8.5% as at the end of 2004. The service sector accounts for 45% of total employment.

Economy

Although relatively small, the economy has been quite resilient to the shocks and impacts of the longstanding ethnic conflict and the tsunami of 2004.

The implementation of the ceasefire agreement with the Tamil rebels in 2001 and the pursuit of a negotiated peace settlement has helped the economy to record positive growth rates.

The economy grew by 5.1% during the first half of 2005 despite the setbacks caused by the tsunami disaster. It is expected to record a growth of 5.3% for 2005. The country's per capita GDP at market prices for the first time crossed the US$1,000 mark in 2004, recording US$1,031.

The services sector is the largest sector in the economy, representing 54% of GDP. Agriculture contributes about 20% and manufacturing 26%. Expatriate worker remittances are a major source of funding the trade deficit.

The capital account is closed but the current account is partly liberalized. The local currency is determined by market forces. Since May 2004 a rising trend in inflation has been observed with substantial demand pressure still prevailing. The year-end inflation is projected to be 10%–11% based on improved supply-side factors and monetary policy measures, though the published figures indicate 13%–14% in September 2005.

Interest rates showed an increasing trend in 2005 with the Average Weighted Deposit Rate (AWDR) moving from 5.3% in January to 6.2% in December. Weighted Average Prime Lending rates moved from 9.8% to 12.2% during the corresponding period. The yield on 12-month Treasury Bills increased from 7.65% to 10.4% during the first eight months of 2005. Based on the expected budget deficit in 2006, higher oil prices and the pressure on the local currency, the upward trend in interest rates is likely to continue.

International trade improved significantly with a 12.7% growth in exports, and an 11.3% growth in imports, while services and remittance increased substantially during the first eight months of 2005. Aided by the high growth in remittances and other inflows, the overall balance of payments has turned to a surplus of around US$190 million by the end of the first eight months of 2005. Gross official reserves increased to US$2.2 billion or 3.2 months' of imports in that period. The budget deficit was 5% of GDP (5.4% in 2004).

Prospects for 2006 are promising according to the Central Bank of Sri Lanka, with a projected 6% economic growth. Key structural reforms in the power and telecommunication sectors and the labour markets are being facilitated by the government.

The banking, insurance and equity markets embody the major part of Sri Lanka's financial sector.

Financial Sector

The commercial banking sector constitutes about 65% of the total assets in the financial system. There are 22 commercial banks operating in Sri Lanka, comprising two large state-owned banks, nine private banks and 11 foreign banks. Their total assets as at the end of July 2005 was about US$11.76 billion. The two state banks account for about 48% of the total assets whilst the foreign banks account for 14%. The average growth rate of deposits in the banking system has been around 15% over the last five years. The two state-owned banks – Bank of Ceylon and Peoples Bank – along with Commercial Bank of Ceylon and Hatton National Bank, account for a large chunk of the current market both in terms of deposits and advances. The performance of the banking sector improved during the first half of 2005, as reflected by the growth in capital funds and increased profits of banks. Customer deposits are the main source of funds for banks and constitute about 75% of their liabilities.

The country's financial system is largely a bank-based one, and not really market-based. The capital markets are underdeveloped and have not posed real competition to the banking sector. The low level of financial disintermediation has resulted in high interest spreads for the banks.

Public confidence in the banking system is high as there has been only one bank failure since the country's independence in 1945 – that of Pramuka Bank, a small savings bank, which collapsed in 2002. The new Government has since announced its commitment to resurrect this bank.

Consolidation is gathering momentum in the banking system as the regulators have begun directing banks towards higher capitalization, better risk management practices, higher operational efficiencies and strict internal controls. The banking system is preparing itself to comply with Basel II.

There are 13 licensed insurance companies in Sri Lanka including one Takaful operator (Amãna Takaful). The total premium collected in 2004 amounted to US$239.11 million, while the total assets of the insurance companies amounted to US$705.57 million. The insurance penetration level measured in terms of total gross premium as a percentage of GDP is around 1.5% and the insurance density or per capita premium amounts to US$14.80. This offers a promising growth opportunity for strong insurance companies and banks who can offer bancassurance products.

The Takaful concept in insurance is seeing increasing market acceptance, and two of the largest insurance operators have announced their intention to offer Takaful products to the market in 2006.

The equity market has remained relatively small despite a long period of existence. Market capitalization is about US$6 billion, or 15% of GDP. The largest securities market is government securities.

The Colombo Stock Exchange (CSE) has gained over 27% in 2005 in terms of All Share Price Index. The daily average turnover on the CSE was around US$4.63 million in 2005, with shares of more than 200 companies being traded. The Securities and Exchange Commission of Sri Lanka is the capital market regulator in the country and monitors the CSE.

Scope for Islamic Banking

Islamic banking has been a long-cherished need among Sri Lanka's Muslims since the creation of market awareness in 1997, when Amana entered the market as the pioneering Islamic financial institution offering Shariah compliant deposit and financing products.

There have been other attempts at village and provincial levels to create Islamic fund-type operations, but their success has been limited due to, among other reasons, their being unregistered entities with little professionalism and the absence of a profit motive. Of late, the Ceylinco Group has formed a company that offers PLS-based products to the market.

Amana has led the market both in terms of creating awareness and providing Shariah compliant financial solutions. Whilst the group was able to obtain early regulatory approval to operate its Takaful insurance business, the regulatory approval for a banking licence has taken well over seven years, as it involved fundamental changes to the Banking Act. Amana is now at the head of the queue for a licence to operate as a full fledged Islamic commercial bank.

Following the new legislation, some of the existing conventional banks are expected to open Islamic banking windows with a view to preventing their Muslim customers from migrating to Islamic banks. It is also possible that the market might see a few new entrants to Islamic banking, although the Central Bank has upped the minimum capital requirements for licensing substantially.

The size of the Islamic market is estimated at around US$500 million-US$600 million.

The regulators are becoming alive to the growing Islamic market segment, both local and global, and the global developments and trends in Islamic banking. Some of the key challenges they face in this regard include developing appropriate mechanisms to regulate Islamic banks, facilitating inter-bank transactions and developing relevant inter-bank and treasury instruments for the investment of surplus funds by Islamic banks. Further relevant changes to the fiscal and legislative environments will soon be necessary to facilitate Islamic banking transactions.

Yet another challenge facing the industry is the competency gap in human resources, both at the regulatory and market levels. Islamic bankers and Shariah scholars are scarce resources and are critical success factors to the industry's future growth and development .

All in all, Sri Lanka is an emerging market and the scope for Islamic banking looks both positive and exciting.

(Faizal Salieh is the Managing Director of Amana Investments, Sri Lanka and can be reachable at fsalieh@amana.lk).

8

Settlement of Islamic Banking Disputes in Indonesia

Opportunities and Challenges*

Abdul Rasyid

Looking to the impressive improvement of the Islamic banks in Indonesia, the existence of Basyanas and Religious court as the institution which has authority to settle the disputes of Islamic banking is very impressive. Basyarnas as a non-litigation institution can play important role in resolving disputes of Islamic banking expeditiously, inexpensively, and simply. Its process of reconciliation is indeed attractive to the disputing parties. However, it remains to be seen how it is managed in a professional manner. Its office should not be centralized in Jakarta, but must have branch offices in every province of Indonesia.

* I would like to gratefully acknowledge the valuable contribution and reversion provided by Prof. Dr. Syed Khalid Rashid in preparing this paper.

Source: www.apmf2008.com © Abdul Rasyid. Reprinted with permission. This paper was originally presented at the International Conference on Mediation in the Asia Pacific Constraints and Challenges at IIUM, Kuala Lumpur, 16-18 June, 2008.

A. Introduction

Islamic banking in Indonesia started to operate from 1992 by virtue of the enactment of the Banking Act No. 7/1992; and when Bank Muamalat was established as the first bank which operates in accordance with Islamic principles. The Banking Act No. 7/1992 was amended by Act No. 10/1998, to provide an opportunity to conventional banks to open an Islamic window. Since that time, the growth of Islamic banking in Indonesia has been steady and fast. Presently, there are 3 full-fledged Islamic banks, 19 Shariah Business Units and 92 Shariah Rural Banks. This tremendous growth deserves to be supported by a strong legislation. One allied aspect that deserves attention relates to settlement of disputes in Islamic banking.

In the past, there was confusion on the question of which forum was competent to settle Islamic banking disputes: civil court or religious court. Both regarded themselves to be competent to settle such disputes. But the problem was that the jurisdiction of the civil courts did not extend to *Shari'ah* matters, within which Islamic banking disputes apparently came. On the other hand, the jurisdiction of the religious courts was limited to Personal law matters which did not cover banking disputes, and was confined to a) marriage, b) inheritance, testamentary succession, *hiba* and waqf. There was no possibility of any deviation as the matter was clearly spelled out in section 49 of the Act No. 7 of 1989.

In the absence of an appropriate body to take charge of the settlement of Islamic banking disputes, an initiative was taken by the Indonesia Council of Religious Scholars to set up BAMUI (Indonesian Muamalat Arbitration Body) in 1993. The name of this body was changed in 2003 to Basyarnas (National Shari'ah Arbitration Body). However, due to very poor knowledge of the Islamic law of arbitration possessed by the banks and their banking customer complaints, the National Shari'ah Arbitration Body could not function effectively. The very fact that a dispute cannot be arbitrated unless there is an arbitration agreement between the parties (*i.e.,* the bank and customer) was not fully appreciated by the parties. Consequently, disputes brought for arbitration by both of them were lacking necessary legal foundation and could not thus be legally arbitrated. Any award made in such an arbitration was not enforceable.

As a result of this problem, most of the cases involving Islamic banking disputes continued to be taken to the civil courts, notwithstanding the questionable knowledge of the judges of such courts of matters relating to Islamic banking and finance.[1]

This anomaly was rectified in February 2006 through Law No. 3 of 2006 which amended Law No. 7 of 1989 and expanded the jurisdiction of the Religious courts to cover adjudication of disputes belonging to Islamic economic matters, including Islamic banking.

This expansion arguably enhanced the status and authority of Religious courts as a dispute settlement institution within the judiciary system in Indonesia. Its jurisdiction is now no more confined to the settlement of disputes in the Islamic family law matters, but extended also to the field of Islamic business and economic matters. However, this turns out as another challenge for Religious courts due to the fact of the complexity of Islamic economics matter, and needed more time to be properly absorbed and understood.

With this in mind, this paper tries to analyze the challenge faced by Basyarnas as a non-litigation forum and Religious courts as litigation institutions both of which have been conferred with the competency to settlement of disputes in the area of Islamic banking.

B. Dispute Settlement in Islamic Banking through Arbitration

B1. Basyarnas (National Shariah Arbitration Body)

In Islam, settlement of disputes, especially in the property and private matters through amicable, means (*islah*) is strongly recommended and is regarded as a praiseworthy deed. The Quran, in *Surah Al Nisa ayat* 128 clearly states:

> *"If a wife fears cruelty or desertion on her husband's part, there is no blame on them if they arrange an amicable settlement between themselves; and such settlement is best; even though men's souls are swayed by greed. But if ye do good and practice self-restraint, Allah is well-acquainted with all that ye do".*

Furthermore, Allah also commands Muslims to bring peace when the dispute arises among them. It is stated in the Quran, *Surah Al-Hujurat, ayat 9*:

> *"If two parties among the Believers fall into a quarrel, make ye peace between them: but if one of them transgresses beyond bounds against the other, then fight ye against the one that transgresses until it complies with the command of Allah; but if it complies, then make peace between them with justice, and be fair: for Allah loves those who are fair (and just)".*

Arbitration in Islamic law is known as *tahkim* which literally means to make someone as arbiter (*hakam*) in a dispute. The role of arbitrator is similar to that of a *qadi* (judge). His power of giving an award, and requiring him to have the same qualifications as that of a *qadi,* bring him very near to a judge (*qadi*). Non-Muslims are allowed under Islamic law to have an arbitrator of their own choice and qualifications.[2]

In Indonesia, BAMUI (Indonesian Muamalat Arbitration Body), which has been changed to Basyarnas (National Shariah Arbitration Body)[3], was initiated by MUI (Majelis Ulama Indonesia) Indonesian Council of Religious Scholars, started working from 1 October 1993. The establishment of this Islamic arbitration body is closely related to the growth of Islamic banking and other institutions which operate on Islamic principles. According to HS. Prodjokusumo, the idea to establish BAMUI could not be detached from the context of socio-economic life of Muslims in Indonesia.[4] However, the main objectives behind the establishment of BAMUI are[5]:

1. To provide justice and speedy settlement of *muamalah*/civil disputes which emerge in the area of commerce, industry, finance, service and others;
2. To accept a request which is submitted by the parties in giving a binding opinion in a matter base on their underlying agreement, even where no dispute has arisen.

When the disputing parties agree to take their dispute to Basyarnas, they commit themselves to follow the system and procedure applied by it. Basyarnas has procedural regulations which encompass *inter alia*: the request to perform arbitration, appointment of the arbitrator, procedure for investigation, reconciliation, authentication and giving of the evidence by witnesses, concluding the investigation, decision making, setting aside of award, registration of the award, enforcement of award and determination of the cost of arbitration.

B2. The Role and Competency of Basyarnas in Indonesian Legal System

The role of Basyarnas in a formal sense has strong legitimation in the Indonesian legal system. The law which prevails in Indonesia provides the opportunity and possibility for an independent tribunal outside the court to resolve a dispute among the parties. According to the explanatory note Sec. 3 (1) of the Act No. 14/1970 on Judicial Powers:

"The settlement of a dispute outside the court, based on reconciliation or arbitration is permissible, however, the award of the arbiter only could only be enforced after receiving permission or order of enforcement from the court"

Until 1999, the legal basis to be used for investigation of cases in arbitration in Indonesia were section 615 up to 651 civil procedurel law (*Reglement op de Rechtvordering*) and Section 377 which is revised (Het Herziene Indonesian Reglement, Staatsblad 1941: 44) and Section 705 Reglemen Acara for the state outside Java and Madura (*Rechtsreglement Buitengewesten, Staatsblad* 1971:227). However, after Law No. 30/1999 on Arbitration and Alternative Dispute Resolution was enacted, section 81 of this Act, firmly states that those regulations will not be valid anymore. This means all stipulations pertaining to arbitration, including foreign arbitrations should abide by the Law No. 30 of 1999. However in *lex specialist* the provision related to the implementation of foreign arbitration regulated in Act No. 5/1968 which officially ratify the Convention on the Settlement of Investment Disputes Between States and Nationals of Other States i.e., ICSID Convention, the Decree of President No. 34/1981 on Ratification of New York Convention 1958 and Regulation of Supreme Court No. 1/1990.[6]

According to H M Tahir Azhari, the existence of Islamic Arbitration (Basyarnas) in Indonesia is *condition sine qua non*, and it has strong foundation in Indonesian legal structure.[7] The competency of Basyarnas encompasses all disputes which arise in commerce, industry, finance, service etc. Apart from that, it is able to bestow the binding opinion about the matter before dispute emerges. This binding opinion will be given by the arbiter based on the request of both the parties. In Sec. 5 (1) and (2) Act No. 30 of 1999, it is stated that

"The dispute that can be resolved through arbitration is restricted to commercial disputes only and only to the extent that the rights concerned fall within the full legal authority of the disputing parties to determine"

"The dispute that can not be resolved through arbitration is a dispute that according to regulation could not be reconciled"

If in the agreement the disputing parties agreed to settle their disputes through arbitration, the court has no jurisdiction to investigate and try such cases. Sec. 1 (3) Act No. 30 of 1999 defines an agreement to arbitrate as follows:

"Arbitration agreement shall mean a written agreement in the form of an arbitration clause entered into by the parties before a dispute arises, or a separate written arbitration agreement made by the parties after a dispute arises."

If the case could not be settled through arbitration, it can be settled through the court as the last resort. In this case, the judge should give attention to the decision given by the arbiter while considering the settlement of the disputes.

B3. The Opportunities and Challenges of Basyarnas

The dispute settlement of Islamic banking in the mode of alternative dispute resolution, through Basyarnas, has some advantages, which may be identified as follows:[8]

1. It reposes trust in the parties by placing the dispute settlement in their hands so that they may use this trust in a respectful and responsible manner.
2. The parties place their trust in the arbiter with full confidence that the dispute will be resolved by a person who has the expertise in the field.
3. The process of taking decision through Basyarnas is expeditious, less complicated and inexpensive.
4. As the parties entrust their dispute in voluntary manner for settlement to the trusted person, it naturally implies they have agreed to implement the decision given by the arbiter, as it is the natural outcome of their own agreement in appointing the arbiter. An agreement implies a promise and promises are to be fulfilled.
5. Islamic arbitration process contains reconciliation as its integral component; hence it becomes part of the Basyarnas process.
6. A clear inference which may be drawn from Basyarnas process is that Islamic law to be used as the basic principle in settling disputes in the area of Islamic banking.

Contrary to the points of strength stated above, there are some weaknesses in Basyarnas that should be improved. *First* of such weakness is the lack of professionalism in Basyarnas personnels. Having known that the Islamic banking in Indonesia has been fast developing and it will play significant role in Indonesian national banking industry in the future, not much has been done in the area of human resource development. As the institution which has authority in dispute settlement of Islamic banking, it should be managed in a professional manner and be supported by the professionals. However, the board members of Basyarnas consist of the busy persons who could not bestow full attention to it. This creates a bad influence on its activity and it could not work in maximal manner. The restructuring of Baysarnas with the professional persons is possible.[9] *Secondly*, Baysranas must have its own building, a good administration, and its own secretariat which is always ready to serve the parties at any time, and have to have the qualified arbiters who have the capability to help the disputing parties to resolve their banking disputes in a good manner. *Thirdly*, the Basyarnas has only 4 branch offices in the whole of Indonesia. These are in Provinces of Surabaya, Riau, Lampung and Yogyajarta. Indonesia consists of 31 provinces and Islamic banks have been widespread and exist in all provinces. These limited number of branch offices of course could not accommodate the demands and facilitate good services to the society. In order to solve this problem, the enlargement of networking of Basyarnas office to other provinces is necessary. *Fourth*, Islamic bank and customers are apparently have less understanding about the Basyarnas as the institution which has jurisdiction in resolving Islamic banking disputes. The mutual familiarization of Basynarnas and Bankers, customers, *ulama*, academicians, entrepreneurs and others should be carried out by conducting seminars, training camps, etc. It is hoped this could agenda can improve their understanding of the role of Basyarnas.

C. Dispute Settlement of Islamic Banking in Indonesia Through Litigation

C1. Jurisdiction of Religious Courts

Religious court is one of the judicature bodies in Indonesia. According to section 49 Act No. 7/1989 on Religious Judiciary, Religious Court only has limited powers which is confined to investigate, and to decide cases only in the field of marriage, inheritance, will, bequest, *waqf* and *zakat* among Muslims. However, once the Act No. 7 of 1989 was amended by Act. No. 3 of 2006, the jurisdiction of Religious Court has been expanded to cover the settlement of disputes in Islamic economic matters between Muslims. The meaning of Islamic economic as given in this new Act is: any act or business activity which is undertaken in accordance with Islamic principles which consists of Syariah banks, Syariah micro financing institutions, Syariah insurance, Syariah reinsurance, Syariah portfolio management, Syariah bonds and Medium-term security, Syariah security market, Syariah finance, Syariah pawn broking, Syariah retired fund institutions and Syariah business.[10] In explanation to that section it is mentioned: "what is meant by 'between the Muslims' is persons or legal institutions who under this section voluntarily agreed to be governed by Islamic law rules pertaining to everything which they agreed to do under the jurisdiction of Religious court".

According to Bagir Manan, the competency of Religious court in settling disputes in Islamic economics extends to:[11]

a. A dispute in the field of Islamic economics between any Islamic finance institution (or fund institution) and their costumers.

b. Dispute in the field of Islamic economics between any finance institution and fund institution.

c. Dispute between two Muslim parties in the field of Islamic economics in which the contract firmly states that the activity is carried out based on Islamic principles.

The jurisdiction of Religious court is not limited to Islamic banking only. However, its power encompasses all kinds of institutions which base their activities on Islamic principles. The expansion of this jurisdiction has arguably enhanced the status of religious court as judicial body in Indonesia. But on the other hand, since Religious courts do not have much experience in the settlement of Islamic banking disputes, it has become a big challenge for it too.

C2. Opportunities and Challenges: Dispute Settlement of Islamic Banking in Religious Court

The amendment of Act No. 7 of 1989 by Act No. 3 of 2006 on Religious Judiciary has conferred on the Religious courts a new jurisdiction in which it settles disputes regarding Islamic economic including Islamic banking. This expansion has arguably enhanced the status and the authority of Religious Court as a dispute settlement institution and is considered as wise and appropriate decision because it achieves harmonization between the material law which is based on Islamic principles and Religious court as the representative of Islamic judiciary in Indonesia. The status of religious court is Islamic and its apparatus have good knowledge of Islamic law.

However, the dispute settlement of Islamic banking in Religious court still faces some challenges such as the absence of any regulation or compilation[12] for the guidance of the judges to resolve the Islamic banking disputes of Islamic banking. Furthermore, there are many in Religious courts such as its judges who still have no knowledge of Islamic economic or Islamic business. There is also no special investigation institution available now which has competency and skill in Islamic banking law.[13]

According to Bagir Manan, the decision that was given to the religious courts in settling disputes in Islamic economics matter has been regarded as an appropriate option as well as a wisdom resolution. This will achieve the harmonization between material law in accordance with Islamic principles and Religious court as the representative of Islamic institution. And that also will synchronize by its apparatus that are Muslims which have good knowledge in Islamic law. In addition, the emergence of anxiety on the exclusive delegation of the cases of Islamic economic to Religious court is overly exaggerated. There is wisdom in the government's decision to recognize the Religious court as competent body to settle disputes of Islamic economic among Muslim and also non-Muslims.[14] This wisdom needs a healthy environment to flourish and prosper.

D. Brief Conclusion

Looking to the impressive improvement of the Islamic banks in Indonesia, the existence of Basyanas and Religious court as the institution which has authority to settle the dispute of Islamic banking is very impressive. Basyarnas as non-litigation institution can play important role in resolving disputes of Islamic banking expeditiously, inexpensively, and simply. Its process of reconciliation is indeed attractive to the disputing parties. However, it remains to be seen how it is managed in a professional manner. Its office should not be centralized in Jakarta, but must have branch offices in every province of Indonesia.

Furthermore, the enforcement of exclusive jurisdiction on the religious courts in the field of Islamic economics including Islamic banking, by virtue of the Act No. 3 of 2006, constitutes a huge trust reposed in these courts which was impossible to conceive in the Dutch colonial era. The Religious courts should carry out this trust in as good a manner as possible. It will also enhance the status of Religious courts in Indonesia that it has power and ability to settle disputes not only in the traditional area of marriage, divorce, inheritance, etc. but in the new area of banking and finance also.

(Abdul Rasyid is a Ph D Candidate, Ahmad Ibrahim Kulliyyah of Law, International Islamic University Malaysia. The author can be reached at ochids2001@yahoo.com).

Endnotes

1 Gemala Dewi, Aspek-Aspek Hukum dalam Perbankan dan Perasuransian Syariah di Indonesia, (Jakarta, Kencana, 2004), p. 104

2 Syed Khalid Rashid, *Alternative Dispute Resolution in Malaysia,* (Ahmad Ibrahim Kulliyyah of Law, IIUM, Kuala Lumpur, 2006), p. 34.

3 Basyarnas was established in 2003 and is located in Jakarta. It has some branches in other provinces. Previously, Basyarnas was known as BAMUI (Indonesian Muamalat Arbitration Body) which was established on 21 October 1993 and had a legal status as Foundation (*Yayasan*). Its founding official document was signed by Chairman of MUI (Indonesian Council of Religious Scholars) KH. Hasan Basri and Secretary General HS. Prodjokusumo. BAMUI was set up by MUI based on the decision of Rekernas of MUI (National Working Meeting) in 1992. The changing of name from BAMUI to Basyarnas was decided in MUI National Working Meeting in 2002. In that meeting the legal body status of BAMUI as Foundation (*Yayasan*) was also changed and it became a body under MUI and had become as one of the arms of MUI organization. However, Basyarnas enjoys independent and autonomous status in discharge of its duties and functions.

4 Saleh, Abdul Rahman, Dkk, *Arbitrase Islam di Indonesia,* BAMUI & BMI, Jakarta, 1994. p. 192.

5 Section 4 Anggaran Dasar Yayasan Badan Badan Arbitrase Muamalah Indonesia

6 Gunawan Widjaja and Ahmad Yani, *Hukum Arbitrase*, (Jakarta: PT. Raja Grafindo Persada, 2000), 1st Edition, pp. v-vi.

7 A. Rahmat Rosyadi and Ngatino, *Arbitrase dalam dalam Perpektif Islam dan Hukum Postif,* (Bandung, PT. Citra Aditya Bakti, 2002), p. 117.

8 Rachmadi Usman, *Aspek-Aspek Hukum Perbankan Islam di Indonesia*, (Bandung: PT. Citra Bakit, 2002), p. 105.

9 Mengurangi Benang Kusut Badan Arbitrase Syari'ah Nasional, *www.hukumonline.com*

10 *Sec. 49 (i) Act No. 3/2006.*

11 Abdul Bagir Manan, "Beberapa Masalah Hukum dalam Praktek Ekonomi Syariah" (Some Lega Problems in the Practice of Islamic Economics), *Makalah Diklat Calon Hakim Angkatan-2 di Banten,* 2007, p. 8.

12 Compilation of Syari'ah Economic Law is still in process. The team formed by the Supreme Court which is headed by the Bagir Manar which currently is the chief of Supreme Court. This compilation will contain all aspects of Islamic economic practices, Zakat and Waqf. This compilation will be released at the end of this year as the regulation of the Supreme Court, and would become the guideline for the judges of Religious court in dispute settlement of Islamic economic matters. See "Menguntit Jejak Kompilasi Hukum Syari'ah Ekonomi", *www.hukumonline.com.*

13 Abdul Bagir Manan, "Beberapa Masalah Hukum dalam Praktek Ekonomi Syariah" p. 26.

14 Ibid.

9

Islamic Banks in Jordan
Performance and Efficiency Analysis

Ali Salman Saleh and Rami Zeitun

Islamic banking commenced in Jordan approximately two decades ago. Ever since it has played an important role in financing and contributing to different economic and social sectors in the country. However, there are limited studies on the financial performance of Islamic banks. This paper, therefore, examines and analyzes the Jordanian experience of Islamic banking, focusing on the two largest Islamic banks in the country: the Jordan Islamic Bank for Finance and Investment (JIBFI) and the Islamic International Arab Bank (IIAB), and evaluates these Islamic banks' performance. The paper also sheds some light on the domestic and global challenges that this sector faces. We used a performance evaluation methodology, and conducted profit maximization, capital structure and liquidity tests, and found that both banks' efficiency and ability has increased, both have expanded their investment and activities and played an important role in financing projects in Jordan.

Source: Review of Islamic Economics. The authors acknowledge the permission given by the Review of Islamic Economics for the Reprint of this paper in this book. This is originally published in Review of Islamic Economics, 2007, vol. 11, no. 1, pp. 41-62. Reprinted with permission.

Another interesting finding is that these banks focused on short-term investments, which is often found in most Islamic banking practices. Our research also found that Islamic banks have a high growth in credit facilities and in profitability; and postulates whether this might encourage other banks to adopt the Islamic financial system.

1. Introduction

An Islamic bank is a financial and social institution whose aims, principles and practices comply with the *Shari'ah* rules, and which must avoid charging interest in any of its practices (Ahmed, 2004). The desirability of abolishing fixed interest rates and the Islamization of financial systems were major issues of discussion at the first meeting of the Islamic Organization Conference (IOC) in Jeddah in 1973 (Haqiqi and Pomeranz, 2005). Many Islamic banks were subsequently founded under the profit and loss sharing system (PLS).

According to Haqiqi and Pomeranz (2005) Islamic banking in its modern form went through three phases of development—1972-1975 period. During this period, running from 1972-1975, Islamic banking was associated with a surge in oil revenues and great liquidity, many important events occurred, notably the establishment of IOC and the launch of Dubai Islamic bank in mid-1970s.

In the second phase from 1976 to the early 1980s, Islamic banking spread from the Gulf countries to Malaysia and westward to the UK. Many international and intercontinental institutions were established, such as Islamic banking associations, and consultant bodies to expand their operations.

In the last phase from 1983-to the present, Islamic banking has come of age. The Arab countries were confronted by economic setbacks, for example, slowdowns in oil revenue during the early 1980s, the relative strength of the US dollar, high interest rates in the US, and capital outflow from OPEC countries. Many Arab banks opened branches in the US, Europe, Asia, and other parts of the world. In some countries—Iran, Bahrain, and Sudan, for example—the operations of the entire banking system were converted to the Islamic mode of finance.

Islamic banking practices are spreading all over the globe. According to some estimates, it has grown at an annual rate of 15% over the past five years. Currently there are over 250 institutions managing assets and client money valued at around US$400 billion (AME Info, 2005). The growth of Islamic banks is proof of at least their viability. We should always bear in mind that Islamic banks are part of the banking system in the countries in which they operate and subject to the same rules and regulations.

With the continual growth of Islamic banking in the Arab and Middle East world, the concept was certain to take hold in Jordan. Jordan has a relatively open society, and an experienced and active banking and finance sector that was strengthened by a number of reforms initiated during the 1980s. The most important factor encouraging Islamic banking in Jordan is undoubtedly the fact that 92% of its people (around 6 million) are Muslims, most of whom are keen to obtain competitive financial services that conform to their beliefs. The country was thus well-placed and ready to adopt the Islamic banking concept and develop it further.

Islamic banking in Jordan started approximately two decades ago, with the foundation of its first Islamic bank, the Jordan Islamic Bank for Finance and Investment in 1978. Since then, Islamic banks in the country have grown in number and size, with the establishment of more branches and more Islamic banks such as the Islamic International Arab Bank, and the establishment of other Islamic financial institutions, such as Jordan Islamic Insurance, Islamic Investment House and Jordan Finance House.

Because there have been limited studies of Islamic banking performance in Jordan, this paper aims to examine and analyze the Jordanian experience of Islamic banking by evaluating the performance of Islamic banks in the country which have been operating over the last two decades. The paper also sheds some light on the role of Islamic banking in Jordan in terms of financing and contributing to various economic and social sectors in the country. We also review some of the changes (domestic and global), which are facing this sector.

This paper is organized as follows. Section II provides an overview of the development of the banking industry and Islamic banking in Jordan. Section III, after explaining the methodology and tools for measuring bank performance, reports the results and analysis. Section IV highlights the challenges ahead and prospects for Islamic banking in Jordan. Section V presents a summary and the paper's conclusions.

2. Banking and Islamic Finance in Jordan

The banking system in Jordan has traditionally been dominated by the Central Bank and Amman Financial Market. The Central Bank was established in 1964, and its major role was for note issue, exchange reserves management, and regulation of credit. The bank acted as the fiscal agent for the government, regulated the commercial banking sector, and sponsored the creation of new financial institutions. The banking sector during the 1970s and early 1980s saw loans and deposits more than double. Over the same period, the number of financial institutions tripled as the government encouraged the expansion of banking services as a key driver of its economic development policy. Deposits were attracted from other Arab countries, as well as savings and remittances, which served to supply loans to growing companies in need of capital.

During the 1980s, Jordan was a unique case among the Arab World when the value of its bank assets surpassed its GDP. Commercial bank assets rose from JD1.1 million in 1980 to JD2.3 billion in 1985. Total deposits also increased from about JD800 million to JD1.7 billion. Strict Central Bank consumer credit controls and government success in encouraging savings resulted in annual growth of 7% from 1980 to 1987. The liquid money supply reached about JD900 million during this period, with no significant inflation. But during the mid-1980s, the government became concerned that the banking sector in the country was expanding too rapidly. It was worried that the banks might get into risky lending activity and that excessive competition for assets might drive them to lend to foreign companies instead of local ones. The Central Bank of Jordan, therefore, imposed a moratorium on the establishment of new commercial banks. In 1985 more than 27% of commercial bank credit financed trade, and less than 10% financed corporate investment (JIR, 2005).

The 1980s also saw the government exercise greater regulation of bank activity to counterbalance fluctuating stock values and the rapid expansion of banking. Among the regulations was that banks were required to invest 8% of their deposits in government bills and bonds, and invest at least 15% of their capital in public and mixed-sector corporate equity. The minimum capital requirement was increased to JD5 million.

Binding interest rate ceilings were set on both loans and deposits, and dinar exchange rates were fixed by the Central Bank.

During the late 1980s, 30 major banks and financial institutions operated in the country, among them eight major locally based conventional commercial banks, six foreign banks, two Islamic banks, and a host of smaller or more specialized foreign and domestic financial institutions. The Arab Bank was by far the largest locally based commercial bank, a Palestinian institution that moved to Amman from Jerusalem in 1948. In terms of total assets the Jordan National Bank, the Cairo-Amman Bank, the Jordan-Kuwait bank, and the Petra Bank were the most important local institutions. Foreign banks included Citibank, Grindlays Bank, the Hong Kong-based British Bank of the Middle East, as well as the Iraq's Rafidayn Bank and Egypt's Arab Land Bank. Chase Manhattan left Jordan following the 1984 government-imposed financial regulations (JIR, 2005).

Since 1989 the Central Bank of Jordan (CBJ) has undertaken a number of reforms to make the banking system more secure and competitive, including:

(i) Paid-up capital of Jordanian banks increased to JD 20 million;

(ii) Paid-up capital of foreign banks increased to JD 10 million;

(iii) Banks are required to hold 80% of required reserves at the CBJ;

(iv) Restrictions on the inter-bank foreign exchange market were lifted during 1996;

(v) Restrictions on the flow of trade in foreign currency were removed during 1997; (vi) Main restrictions on foreign capital were removed during 1997 (JIB, 2005); (vii) During 1999-2002, more reforms were undertaken to enhance the sector such as the new banking law, new securities law, new auditing profession law, among others (Khamis, 2003).

The number of banks operating in Jordan rose to 24 at the end of 2004, of which 14 were commercial, eight foreign banks and two Islamic banks (Central Bank of Jordan, 2004). In addition to that, there are four specialized credit institutions in Jordan (such as Industrial Development Bank etc). These banks carry out business throughout the Kingdom through a network of 447 branches and 154 representative offices. Thus, the population branch index of operating banks, at the end of 2004, was nearly 11.9 thousand citizens per branch. On the other hand, the number of branches of Jordanian banks operating abroad reached 124, of which 52 branches were operating in Palestine in addition to ten representative offices (Central Bank of Jordan, 2004). It is also worth noting here that the Amman Stock Exchange (ASE) was established in 1976, and is considered to be the most efficient stock exchange in the Arab World, as well as the largest and fastest growing market in the region open to investors. The ASE is one of the few Middle East and North African countries (MENA) markets which take part in the International Finance Corporation Emerging Markets Index. Its market capitalization to GDP ratio of 73.1% is one of the highest in the region, exceeding that of many countries such as Israel, Saudi Arabia, Egypt, among others (JIB, 2005).

3. The Structure of Islamic Banking in Jordan

Currently there are two Islamic banks listed in the Amman Stock Exchange (ASE): namely Jordan Islamic Bank for Finance and Investment and Islamic International Arab Bank PLC.

3.1 The Jordan Islamic Bank for Finance and Investment (JIBFI)

The Jordan Islamic Bank for Finance and Investment was established as a public shareholding company in 1978, and was licensed with the objective to practice financing, banking and investment activities in compliance with the provisions of *Shari'ah* law. It has succeeded in achieving substantial growth (Table 1) and, by providing all kinds of investment activities, has established itself as one of the leading banks in Jordan.

JIBFI plays an effective role in developing economic and social activities, as evidenced by the growing number of people who deposit their savings with the bank. The bank channels these deposits into investment and job-creation. The number of people who benefited from interest free loans reached about 144,000, and the total value of such loans amounted to JD 51.1 million. Given the objective of the bank to increase its presence in the country so as to reach all citizens interested in using Islamic banking products (such as *Mudaraba, Musharka, Murabaha, etc.),* it spreads its network, which comprised 52 branches and 12 cash offices. By 2004, the number of accounts opened with the bank through its network reached 997,000; the number of its employees reached 1418 in 2004. Also, it has been successful in establishing correspondent relations with more than 300 international banks (JIBFI, Annual Report, 2004).

Table 1: Jordan Islamic Bank for Finance and Investment (JIBFI) Aggregates during 1998-2003						
	1998	**1999**	**2000**	**2001**	**2002**	**2003**
Total Assets	706.763	657.562	658.892	703-843	797-012	975-490
Direct Credit Facilities, Net	391-594	277-572	250.958	252.571	281.369	321.983
Customers Deposits	534.821	547-794	564-577	621.509	710.520	876.956
Total Shareholders Equity	50.910	52.588	54-529	53-578	55-592	56.983
Growth (%)						
Total Assets	–	-6.9614	0.2022	6.8223	13-2371	22.3935
Direct Credit Facilities, Net	–	-29.1176	-9.5880	0.6427	11.4020	14-4343
Customers Deposits	–	2.4257	3.0638	10.0839	14.3218	23-4245
Total Shareholders Equity	–	3-2965	3-6899	-1-7430	3-7575	2.5022
Source: Central Bank of Jordan and Amman Stock Exchange.						

Table 2: Islamic International Arab Bank Aggregates during 1998-2003						
	1998	**1999**	**2000**	**2001**	**2002**	**2003**
Total Assets	137.294	216.321	197.036	253.246	314.741	385-529
Direct Credit Facilities, Net	85.982	145-747	55-174	97.063	105.927	122.670
Customers Deposits	94.408	169.233	77.361	112.436	152.328	197-594
Total Shareholders Equity	40.610	42.025	45-177	45-559	47.085	48.917
Growth (%)						
Total Assets		57.561	-8.915	28.528	24.282	22.491
Direct Credit Facilities, Net		69.509	-62.144	75-922	9-133	15.806
Customers Deposits		79-257	-54.287	45-339	35.480	29.716
Total Shareholders Equity		3.484	7-500	0.846	3-349	3-892
Source: Central Bank of Jordan and Amman Stock Exchange						

3.2 The Islamic International Arab Bank (IIAB)

The Islamic International Arab Bank (IIAB) is the second bank in Jordan to operate according to Islamic *Sharīᶜah.* It began its operations in February 1998 with four branches in Jordan. It is offering a complete set of Islamic banking, financing and correspondence services to meet economic and social needs within the banking sector in accordance with the *Sharīᶜah.* IIAB is now ranked as the fourth bank in Jordan with a paid-up capital of 40 JD million (1JD = US$1.429). At the end of 2002 it had eleven branches around the country, and 217 employees. Table 2 summarizes the banks aggregates during the period 1998-2003 (IIAB, 2002).

4. Methodology and Performance Analysis of Islamic Banks in Jordan

According to financial management theory, banks' performance can be evaluated using various financial ratios, for example, profitability ratios and liquidity ratios, among others. Sabi (1996) and Samad (1999), among others, have used such financial ratios to evaluate or analyze bank performance. In this study, 'Banking Efficiency Model' will be used to measure the performance of Islamic banking in Jordan. Due to unavailability of long-period time-series data for IIAB, the study is limited only to four years time-series data. Even so, since there have been no studies on the development of Islamic banks in Jordan, the evaluation done here should be of some use.

Performance evaluation is an important step to measure the growth and development of any bank. It is customary in commercial banks to evaluate their objectives and goals. The core objective of banks, as of most commercial institutions, is to maximize profits. Without making profits, firms are unable to continue working and develop services. On the other hand, Islamic banks also have other objectives besides making or maximizing profits, namely to foster economic and social well-being and to ensure that there is no exploitation of the customers.

4.1 Profit Maximization Test

Eight indicators of profitability and performance are taken to evaluate the bank performance as depicted in Table 3 and Table 4.

Table 3: Profitability and Performance for JIBFI

Profitability and Performance	2000	2001	2002	2003
Return on Assets (ROA) (%)	0.33	0.14	0.26	0.33
Return on Equity (ROE) (%)	3.95	1.88	3.68	5.62
Net Profit and Commissions Income/Operational Income (%)	88.41	86.31	90.37	87.44
Credit Profit/Credit Facilities, Net (%)	11.89	10.75	10.15	10.09
Net Income/Total Revenues (%)	6.38	3.18	5.89	7.95
Total Revenues/Total Assets (%)	5.12	4.50	4.37	4.13
(Provision for Credit Facilities + Profit in Suspense)/Credit Facilities (%)	9.95	10.65	11.01	6.86
Net Income/Total Liabilities	**0.36**	**0.16**	**0.28**	**0.35**

These analyses in Tables 3 and 4 demonstrate that both measures of performance (ROA and ROE) are positive for both banks. Both measures of performance are higher in IIAB in all years, compared with JIBFI. The ROA in 2000 was 0.33% JIBFI compared with 1.59% for IIAB. The ROE in 2000 was 3.95% for JIBFI, compared with 6.94% for IIAB.

Table 4: Profitability and Performance for IIAB

Profitability and Performance	2000	2001	2002	2003
Return on Assets (ROA) (%)	1.59	1.14	0.58	0.52
Return on Equity (ROE) (%)	6.94	6.33	3.88	4.08
Net Profit and Commissions Income/Operational Income (%)	33.43	44.21	62.50	60.20
Credit Profit/Credit Facilities, Net (%)	8.95	6.68	6.39	5.66
Net Income/Total Revenues (%)	32.03	26.75	18.66	19.30
Total Revenues/Total Assets (%)	4.97	4.25	3.11	2.68
(Provision for Credit Facilities + Profit in Suspense)/Credit Facilities (%)	1.43	1.48	1.40	1.51
Net Income/Total Liabilities	**2.06**	**1.39**	**0.68**	**0.59**

Figures 1 and 2 show the ROI and ROE for JIBFI from 1989 to 2003. The bank's ROI decreased during 1991, 1997, 1999, 2001, and 2002. The decrease during the years 1999, 2001 and 2002 might be due to competition between the two Islamic banks, while the decrease during 1991 could be because of the First Gulf War.

Figure 1: Return on Investment (ROI) for JIBFI

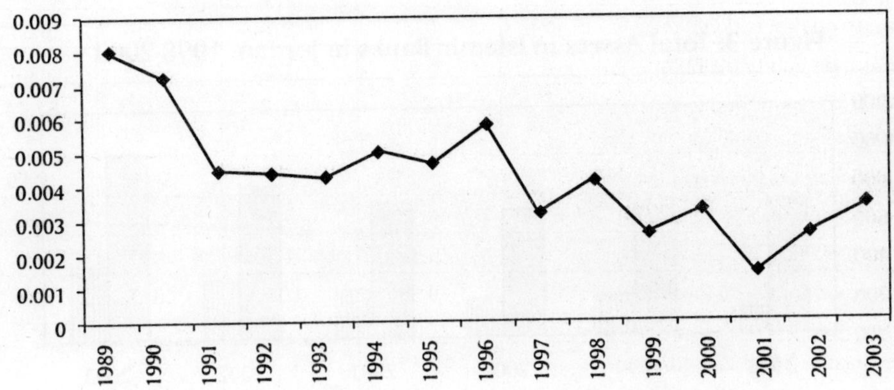

Source: Amman Stock Exchange and JIBFI.

Figure 2: Return on Equity (ROE) for JIBFI

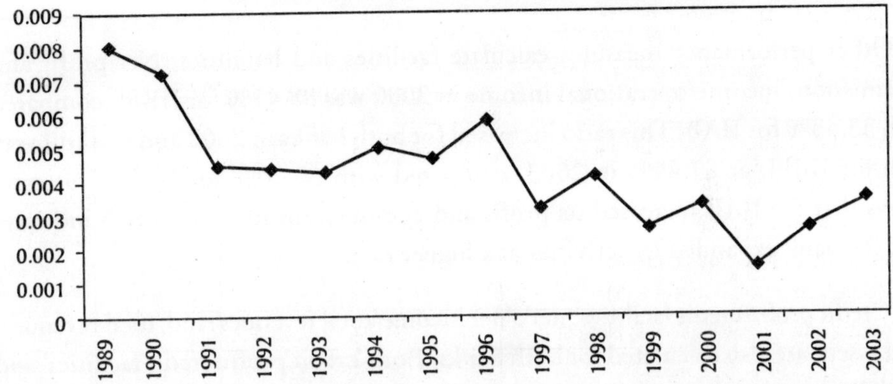

Source: Amman Stock Exchange and JIBFI.

The bank performance measure ROA declined for both banks in 2001. While it increased for JIBFI in 2002 and 2003, it continued to decrease for IIAB. However, ROA was still higher for the IIAB than for JIBFI.

Figure 3 shows that the total assets held by JIBFI were more than the total assets held by IIAB in the years studied: approximately 461.856 million in 2000 and 589,961 million in 2003. Also, the total shareholder equity in JIBFI is greater than the total shareholder equity in IIAB—approximately 9.352 million, compared with 8.065 million in 2003.

Figure 3: Total Assets in Islamic Banks in Jordan, 1998-2003

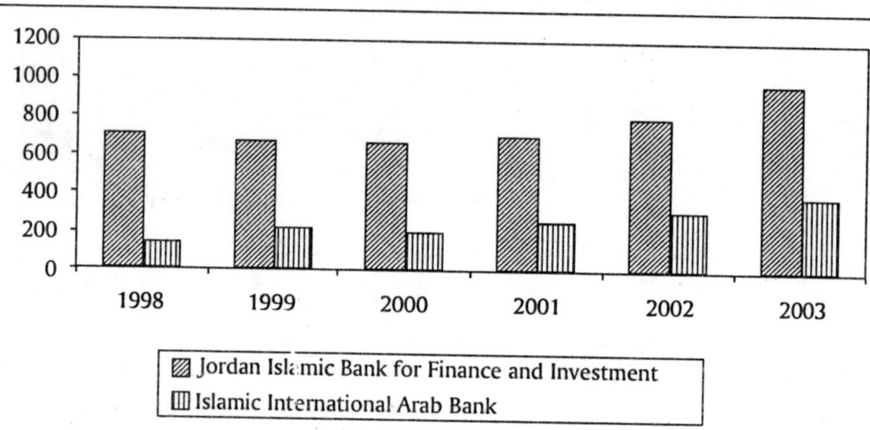

Source: Amman Stock Exchange.

Other performance measures calculate facilities and liabilities. Net profit and commissions income/operational income in 2000 was 88.41% for JIBFI, compared with 33.43% for IIAB. This ratio increased for both banks in 2002 and was still very high for JIBFI, at 87.44% in 2003, compared with 60.20% for IIAB. This ratio shows that the IIAB increased its profit and commissions income, which indicates that the bank expanded its activities at a higher rate.

'Credit profit/credit facilities, net', 'net income/total revenues' and 'total revenues/ total assets' are also calculated for both banks. Both 'credit profit/credit facilities' and 'total revenues/total assets' are higher for JIBFI, compared with IIAB (see Table 3 and Table 4). For example, the ratio of 'Credit Profit/Credit Facilities' for JIBFI was 11.89% in 2000 compared with 8.95% for IIAB.

The Net Income/Total Revenues ratio for JIBFI was 6.38% in 2000 compared with 32.03% for IIAB. This ratio increased in 2003 to 7.95% for JIBFI and decreased for IIAB to 19.30%, which could be due to increased administration expenses resulting from expansion and opening of new branches.

Figure 4: Earning per Share (EPS) for JIBFI

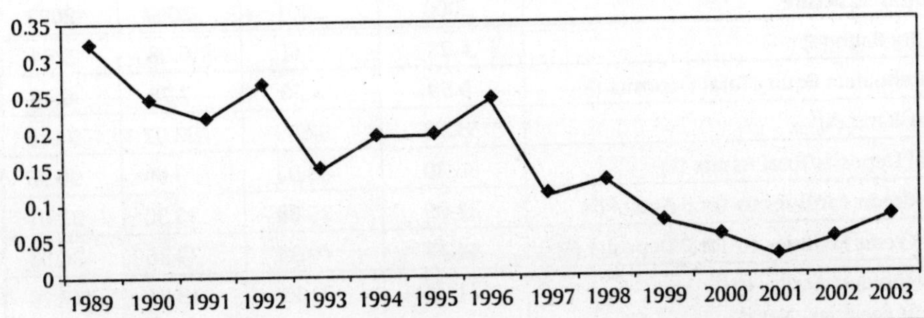

Source: Amman Stock Exchange.

Another ratio, the provision for credit facilities + profits in suspense/credit facilities ratio, was very high for the JIBFI, compared with the same period for IIAB. For example, this ratio was 6.86% in 2003 for JIBFI, compared with 1.51% for IIAB. Net income/total liabilities was lower for JIBFI compared with IIAB.

Another measure used to evaluate bank performance is bank earning per share (EPS). Figure 4 shows that this ratio for JIBFI decreased during the last six years measured.

Overall, the above performance measures show the ability and the efficiency of both Islamic banks to increase their income and reduce expenses.

4.2 Capital Structure

The importance of capital structure analysis is that it reflects bank risk, and also shows the structure of bank loans and deposits, as well as to what degree the bank is able to face an emergency such as a demand deposit. Furthermore, it determines what types of investment the banks concentrate on, and whether the bank prefers to invest in long-term or short-term investments.

Tables 5 and 6 show ten ratios to measure the capital structure of the Islamic banks. The equity ratio reflects the total equity/total assets. For JIBFI the equity ratio decreased to 5.84% in 2003 compared to 8.28% in 2000; for IIAB, it declined to 12.69% in 2003 compared to 22.93% in 2000. The lower equity ratio for JIBFI reflects the expansion of this bank in total assets. The higher equity ratio for IIAB indicates that the bank was expanding its investments.

Table 5: Capital Structure for JIBFI

Capital Structure	2000	2001	2002	2003
Equity Ratio (%)	8.28	7.61	6.98	5.84
Shareholders Equity/Total Deposits (%)	9.59	8.56	7.78	6.46
Debt Ratio (%)	91.72	92.39	93.02	94.16
Total Deposits/Total Assets (%)	86.30	88.95	89.69	90.36
Net Credit Facilities to Total Assets (%)	38-09	35.88	35.30	33.01
Net Credit Facilities to Total Deposits (%)	44.13	40.34	39.36	36.53
Shareholders Equity to Credit Facilities, Net (%)	21.73	21.21	19.76	17.70
Current Assets/Total Assets	39.467	41.121	40.328	51.041
Total Debt/Total Equity	1,108.33	1,213.67	1,333.69	1,611.91

Table 6: Capital Structure for IIAB

Capital Structure	2000	2001	2002	2003
Equity Ratio (%)	22.93	17.99	14.96	12.69
Shareholders Equity/Total Deposits (%)	31.47	23.48	18.64	15.29
Debt Ratio (%)	77.07	82.01	85.04	87.31
Total Deposits/Total Assets (%)	72.87	76.61	80.24	82.97
Net Credit Facilities to Total Assets (%)	28.00	38.33	33.66	31.82
Net Credit Facilities to Total Deposits (%)	38.43	50.03	41.95	38.35
Shareholders Equity to Credit Facilities, Net (%)	81.88	46.94	44.45	39.88
Current Assets/Total Assets	48.12	51.07	49.40	50.14
Total Debt/Total Equity	336.14	455.87	568.46	688.12

The shareholder equity/total deposit measure reflects the percentage of total equity to total deposit. This decreased from 9.59% in 2000 to 6.46% in 2003 for JIBFI, which also decreased from 31.47% to 15.29% for IIAB during the same period. This decrease reflects the increase in customers' deposits. As seen from the tables, JIBFI increased its deposits from 2000 until 2003 at a higher rate.

The debt ratio for both banks is very high because of a high percentage of customer deposits, and because each bank depends on customer deposits to lend money. The debt ratio increased from 91.72% in 2000 to 94.16% in 2003 for JIBFI, and also increased from 77.07 per cent in 2000 to 87.31% in 2003 for IIAB. Tables 5 and 6 show that both banks increased their debt ratio over the years analyzed. The results in the previous ratio are explained by the ratio of total deposits/total assets ratio. This ratio shows the growth of deposits in both banks. Both ratios (net credit facilities to total assets and net credit facilities to total deposits) for JIBFI decreased in 2003 in comparison with 2000, 2001 and 2002. Both ratios increased for IIAB in 2003 (see Tables 5 and 6).

Figure 5: Credit to Deposit Ratio for Jordan Islamic Bank for Finance and Investment

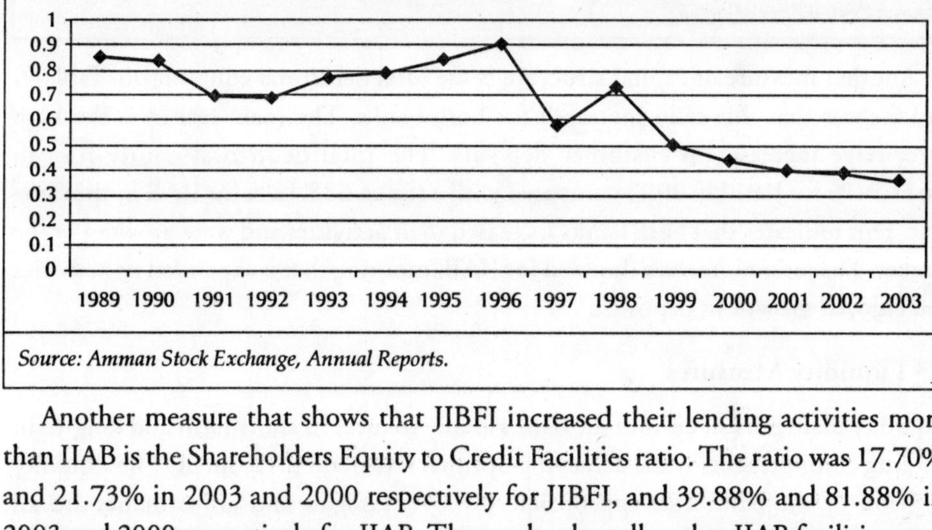

Source: Amman Stock Exchange, Annual Reports.

Another measure that shows that JIBFI increased their lending activities more than IIAB is the Shareholders Equity to Credit Facilities ratio. The ratio was 17.70% and 21.73% in 2003 and 2000 respectively for JIBFI, and 39.88% and 81.88% in 2003 and 2000 respectively for IIAB. The results also tell us that IIAB facilities were growing at a higher rate. Figure 5 indicates that the credit to deposits ratio decreased in the last five years for JIBFI. This could be as a result of a higher increase in deposits compared with low increase in credit. Figure 6 shows that the yearly credit issued by JIBFI increased from 1989 to 2004. The credit facilities increased during the last 15 years, which reflects the bank's growth in credit in the Jordanian market.

The current assets/total assets ratio reflects the structure of assets, as a measure of liquidity. This ratio increased in both banks—from 39.467% in 2000 to 51.041% in 2003 for JIBFI, for example. This increase is due to the increase in the bank's deposits as well as other assets in which the bank expanded its investment in facilities. This suggests that JIBFI focuses on short-term rather than long-term investment.

Figure 6: Yearly Islamic Bank Credit for JIBFI

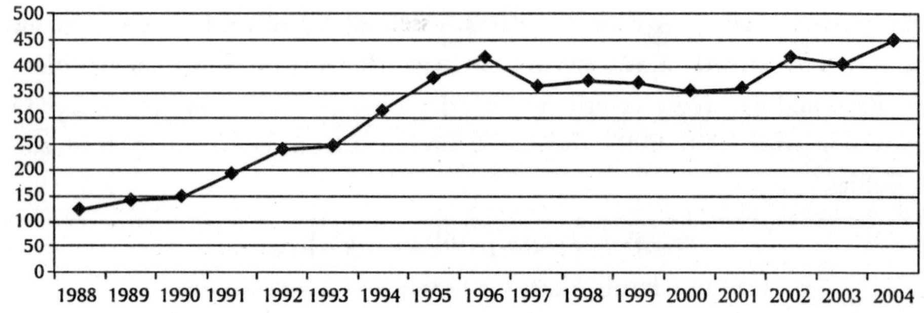

Source: Central Bank of Jordan.

Another measure of capital structure is the total debt/total equity ratio. Tables 5 and 6 show that this ratio increased for both banks. The main reason is the high percentage increases in customer deposits. The total debt/total equity rose to 1,611.91% for JIBFI in 2003 compared with a rise to 688.12% for IIAB in the same year. This indicates that both banks increased their activities and were growing in the market. The ratio more than doubled for IIAB, meaning that it expanded its activities and enjoyed growth in deposits.

4.3 Liquidity Measures

Liquidity management ensures the bank's ability to meet its short-term and long-term funding commitments while achieving optimal return on investment. The liquidity position of the bank and appropriate policy strategies and adjustments are an important element of its position and ability to expand and issue loans, and expand its investment activities. Liquidity analysis at different levels including a maturities analysis of assets and liabilities is important for banks to be confident about their liquidity. Such analysis also covers the source and use of funds.

As discussed earlier, the capital structure of both Islamic banks became stronger and more dependent on short-term rather than long term investment. The structure of its capital affects the liquidity risk. To measure that risk and the bank's ability to meet its obligations, three measures of liquidity are taken. Tables 7 and 8 summarize these ratios in both banks. JIBFI increased its quick ratio in 2003 to 0.56% from 0.46% in 2000. The quick ratio in IIAB was higher, going to 0.60% in 2003 from 0.66% in 2000.

The ratio of cash and investments to total deposits was close to 65% in both banks in 2003. The increase indicates that there was a growing rate of lending. It also reflects the banks' ability to cover loans from assets as well as to face instant demand for deposits. Both banks have the ability to meet instant demand for money.

Another measure of liquidity is the Cash + Trading Investments/ Total Deposits ratio. This ratio for IIAB was higher than for JIBFI.

Table 7: Bank Liquidity, JIBFI

Liquidity ratios	2000	2001	2002	2003
Quick Ratio (Times)	0.46	0.46	0.45	0.56
Cash + Investments/Total Deposits (%)	61.94	64.31	56.78	65.13
Cash + Trading Investments/ Total Deposits (Times)	0.46	0.47	0.45	0.56

Table 8: Bank Liquidity, IIAB

Liquidity ratios	2000	2001	2002	2003
Quick Ratio (Times)	0.66	0.67	0.62	0.60
Cash + Investments/Total Deposits (%)	66.04	66.67	64.23	64.75
Cash + Trading Investments/ Total Deposits (Times)	0.66	0.67	0.62	0.60

5. Challenges and Prospects of Islamic Banking in Jordan

The Islamic banking industry has grown rapidly worldwide since the 1970s, and has become an important issue for bankers, researchers and policy makers. It has grown rapidly in the Middle East and in Jordan in particular, because the country has an open and active society and is one of the most experienced banking sectors in the Arabic region. The country's majority Muslim population, most of whom are professionals and businessmen, are keen to obtain competitive financial services that meet their beliefs. These factors have created a conducive environment and opportunities for the country to be engaged in Islamic banking concepts for the last two decades.

Islamic banks in Jordan have great potential to grow further in the coming years, because they are focusing on many strategies to attract more customers from Muslim as well as non-Muslim areas, and are enhancing their marketing activities by increasing the awareness of their type of banking services and strengthening the relationship with customers. Islamic banks in Jordan are trying to build a solid, long-term relationship between Islamic banking providers and customers. Islamic banks in Jordan have great potential to attract foreign capital investment from other Muslim and neighbouring Arab and Middle Eastern countries, especially after September 11. This will naturally assist the development of the county's economy.

Table 9: Elements of the Financing and Investment Portfolio for IIAB

	1999	2000	2001	2002
Murabahah	16,711,772	29,314,743	49,087,017	46,274,243
Mudarabah	279,366	1,311,785	1,052,426	2,905,134
Mushdrakah	-	325,284	626,993	605,132
Istisna'	755,928	1,390,300	1,151,330	936,531
Specified Commodities Investments	69,502,530	121,216,710	163,260,477	137,105,390
Customers' Liabilities – Letters of Credit	4,404,745	8,368,316	5,878,097	6,231,320
Customers' Liabilities – Letters of Guarantee	1,173,921	1,856,350	2,443,216	3,736,371
Acceptances	682,084	1,898,128	2,546,015	4,061,085

Source: IIAB (2002)

Islamic banks in Jordan have played an important role in financing and developing various sectors in the Jordanian economy by using elements of the Islamic approach to banking (see Table 9), such as *Musharakah, Mudarabah, Murabahah Istisnāᶜ*, among many others. Table 10 shows how the Islamic International Arab Bank has contributed to various sectors in the economy, such as industry and mining, agriculture, construction, trade and others. Where most of these sectors are in urgent need for finance, Islamic banks have played an important role in financing business operations, improving their business performance and creating jobs in the labour market. This is of course true for other Islamic banks in the country, but especially so for the Jordan Islamic Bank, as shown in Table 11, where its contribution to various sectors and thus its commitment to its social role are evidenced. For example, the Jordan Islamic Bank has continued its programme for financing small-scale industries. Since the start of this programme, the bank has financed nearly 40 projects, with a cumulative cost of approximately JD 700,500 (JIBFI, 2003). Table 11 shows the bank's contribution to different sectors of the Jordanian economy. This covers a wide range of social activities and utilities, including hospitals, medical clinics, education, transport and many others.

Table 10: Contribution of Islamic Banking in the following Sectors— IIAB

Sector	1999	2000	2001	2002
Industry and Mining	1,618,631	2,165,131	2,070,024	2,527,679
Agriculture	205,732	525,747	590,980	711,323
Construction	795,328	1,034,227	4,158,566	4,946,451
General Trade	9,068,609	7,592,845	12,993,493	9,6l3,8ll
Transportation Services	674,874	504,756	289,578	108,346
Properties, Real Estate Financing	2,048,528	5,074,269	7,959,681	8,881,677
Automobile Financing	i,34i,555	3,151,534	7,421,749	7,980,575
Consumer Goods Financing	1,924,993	9,545,582	9,871,763	9,355,737
Others	370,536	3,081,791	6,561,932	6,595,441

Source: IIAB (2002).

Table 11: Contribution of JIBFI in Various Economic Sectors 2002-2003

Sectors	2002 (JD '000)	2003 (JD '000)
Agriculture	1,070	1,261
Industry and Mining	31,496	33,420
General Trade	55,205	95,072
Construction	113,832	116,770
Transport	45,645	57,137
Miscellaneous	233,143	168,638
Total	480,391	472,298

Source: JIBFI (2003)

Islamic banks in Jordan have the potential to increase their customer base to cover most of the country by opening new branches and offices in order to be near to current as well as potential customers. The banks are working hard to achieve these goals, despite the strong local challanges and the difficult circumstances facing this sector. The banks nevertheless have the potential to grow further and to enhance development in production sectors, as evidenced by the bank's record of performance and its strategies. Among these are—maintaining the strength of the banks' financial position, increasing the Islamic banks' market share, optimizing the profits of shareholders and depositors, increasing adherence to ethical values and improving performance standards.

Islamic banks in Jordan are trying to adopt all the necessary tools and other means to achieve their goals by increasing their customer base, increasing the awareness of Islamic banking products, adopting new financial and investment tools, adopting IT to provide the best services for its customers, providing training for its employees and many other means important for their development and performance. Islamic banks in Jordan have good support from both the public as well as private sectors. These banks have the potential to succeed by providing distinguished banking and investment services that satisfy government and private institutions as well as individuals, and will play an important role in strengthening the Jordanian banking sector as well as the economy as a whole.

Even though the Islamic banks in Jordan are performing well and have solid plans for the future, they also face some key challenges domestically as well as globally that reduce their growth potential. Among these are the conflict situations in the region (for example, the political turmoil in Palestine and other parts of the Middle East), the economic slowdown that has plagued the country for the past few years, globalization (for example, abolition of tax barriers, liberalization of commodities and services and so on), increased cash surpluses with limited finance and investment opportunities (IIAB, 2002), public awareness and acceptance, lack of institutions that conduct research and development in this area, lack of skilled professional people, and local competition from large numbers of commercial banks operating in the country.

Islamic banking globally also faces many challenges. Saleh and Zeitun (2005) identify many for Lebanon, such as public awareness and acceptance, high competition from many conventional banks, lack of talented labour, among others. Islamic banking also faces financial globalization, speculation, the flow of savings abroad, competition from international banks (AME, 2005), lack of an inter-bank Islamic money market and Islamic money brokers, investors who are unwilling to hold to maturity Islamic paper with a long-term nature, different interpretation by Islamic scholars in different countries (AME, 2005) and so on. Banks also face problems regarding their readiness to meet global competition (due to their limited capital and asset base) and shortage of skilled and trained labour in the Islamic banking industry, the defaulting culture of borrowers, a lack of harmonization of Islamic financial practices, confusion about what is acceptable practice in the Islamic banking industry and many other challenges (Sarker, 1999; Saleh and Zeitun, 2005). Further, Islamic banking must concentrate on risk management and product innovation. The issue of human capital also needs greater attention, and development is required to meet the needs of more diversified business activities.

6. Conclusion

While Islamic banks in Jordan have been operating for the last two decades, there have been limited studies on their financial performance. To fill this gap, this paper has analyzed and evaluated the Jordanian experience with Islamic banking in order to determine the Islamic banks' performance as well as their activities. The paper also reviewed the domestic and global challenges that are facing this relatively new concept.

By using performance evaluation procedures, which are important to measure the growth and development of any bank, we found that both the IIAB and JIBFI banks showed that their efficiency and the profitability increased. Both banks expanded their investments and activities and have played significant roles in financing important projects in the market. These Islamic banks had a high growth in credit facilities and profitability.

Additional interesting findings were that these Islamic banks have focused on short- rather than long-term investments. This seems to be the case for most Islamic banking practices, where the capital structure becomes stronger and depends on short-term investment. In comparing the two banks, the Jordan Islamic Bank for Finance and Investment has increased its lending activities more than the Islamic International Arab Bank, and the facilities of the latter also grew at a higher rate. The results also show that the Jordan Islamic Bank for Finance and Investment has a high profitability, which should encourage other banks to employ financial Islamic products.

Islamic banking in Jordan has played an important role in financing and contributing to various sectors in the country, such as industry and mining, agriculture, construction, trade and others. Most of these sectors are in urgent need of finance, so

Islamic banks' investments here show their commitment to their social role. They have played an important role in financing business operations, improved their own business performance and created jobs in the labour market.

The paper also sheds some light on the development of Islamic banking globally. This sector has not only grown in the Muslim world, but has also gained significant attention in the Western world, with over 250 Islamic banks worldwide controlling approximately US$400 billion in assets and client money. The growth of these banks is proof of their success, and an indication that these banks continue to grow in number and size worldwide.

Islamic banks in Jordan are facing many challenges, among them, conflicts in the region, the economic slowdown, globalization, increased cash surpluses with limited finance and investment opportunities, public awareness and acceptance, lack of institutions that conduct research and development in this area, lack of skilled and professional people, and local competition from large numbers of commercial banks that are operating in the country.

Since the majority of the population in Jordan are Muslims, and given the promising and positive factors in the Islamic banking system, the future of Islamic banks in the country seems promising, and they could emerge as major financial institutions in the region. However, in order to ensure continuous success, Islamic banks need to have good corporate governance, and invest in IT and innovation, in order to increase their competitiveness. They should adopt more strategies to promote their products and establish long-term relationships with customers. Public awareness needs to be increased, and customers need to understand the Islamic financial concepts much better in order to trust and utilize these banks' products. Therefore, Islamic banks have to work harder to brand their products and to build a good relationship with customers.

The management of Islamic banks must also ensure that staff has the necessary skills and knowledge about Islamic banking products and principles. There is a need for more collaboration between Islamic banks in Jordan, as well as with other Islamic banks in the Arab and Muslim world, to increase and open up more Islamic banking training centres and develop institutions that conduct research and development to improve the work of Islamic banks.

Jordan needs to lead collaboration with other countries that are embracing this concept, such as Dubai, Bahrain, Malaysia and others, in order to exchange ideas and knowledge and work on issues such as the application of universal banking, crisis management and developing an Islamic financial market (especially for medium- and long-term products). In order to eliminate confusion and develop a more comprehensive Islamic banking system, the development of the securitization process, *Sharīᶜah* harmonization, product standardization and the application of *Sharīᶜah*-compliant products are also needed.

These banks should always be ready to adopt new, and enhance their existing, IT and other skills to maintain efficiency and productivity, in order to be customer oriented, and innovative in terms of products to meet the requirements of more diversified business activities.

This paper used performance evaluation methodology to examine the Jordanian experience in Islamic banking, and found that the efficiency and ability of Islamic banks in Jordan have expanded, and that they have played an important role in financing many investment projects in the country. Islamic banks in Jordan have achieved high growth levels in terms of profitability and credit expansion, which should encourage other banks to operate under and practice Islamic banking principles based on *Sharīᶜah* rules.

Because there are very limited studies in the area of Islamic banking in Jordan, this study is an important first step towards understanding the development of Islamic banking in the Middle East, and in Jordan in particular. This study can also be extended to compare the performance of Jordanian Islamic banks with conventional ones by using more sophisticated techniques such as panel data regression models or Data Envelopment Analysis (DEA).

(Ali Salman Saleh, Lecturer in Economics at the School of Economics, University of Wollongong, Australia. The author can be reached at Ali.Saleh@vu.edu.au, and

Rami Zeitun, Lecturer in Finance at the School of Economics and Finance, University of Western Sydney, Australia. The author can be reached at rami.zeitun@qu.edu.qa respectively.)

References

Ahmed, M. (2004). *Islamic versus Traditional Banking in the Arab Region: Premises and Promises.* Paper presented to the International Seminar on The Prospects of Arab Economic Cooperation, Alexandria, Egypt.

AME Info (2005). *Islamic Investment and Finance Set to Grow Despite Challenges.* Available at: <*Url: http://www.ameinfo.com*>.

Amman Stock Exchange (1990). *Annual Report.* Amman, Jordan

Amman Stock Exchange (1995). *Annual Report.* Amman, Jordan

Amman Stock Exchange (2002). *Annual Report.* Amman, Jordan

Amman Stock Exchange (2003). *Annual Report.* Amman, Jordan

Amman Stock Exchange (2004). *Annual Report.* Amman, Jordan

Central Bank of Jordan (2000). *Annual Report.* Amman, Jordan

Central Bank of Jordan (2004). *Annual Report,* Amman, Jordan

Central Bank of Jordan (2005). *Yearly Statistical Series* (1964-2003 J. Amman, Jordan

Haqiqi, A. W. and Pomeranz, F. (2005). *Accounting Needs of Islamic Banking,* Available at: <*Url: http://islamic-finance.net/islamic-ethics/artcilei2.html*>, Access date: 10th October, 2005.

Haron, S. and Yamiruleng, K. (2003). "Islamic Banking in Thailand: Prospects and Challenges", *International Journal of Islamic Financial Services,* 5 (2).

IBF NET (2004, September). *Islamic Banks and Financial Institutions.* Available at: <*Url: htt://islamic-finance.net*>.

IIAB – Islamic International Arab Bank (2002). *Annual Report.* Amman, Jordan IIAB – Islamic International Arab Bank (2004). *Annual Report.* Amman, Jordan

JIB – Jordan Investment Bank (2005). *Finance and Banking.* Available at: <*Url: http://www.jordaninvestment.com/2c.htm*>, Access Date: 9th September 2005.

JIBFI – Jordan Islamic Bank for Finance and Investment (2003). *Annual Report.* Amman, Jordan.

JIBFI – Jordan Islamic Bank for Finance and Investment (2004). *Annual Report.* Amman, Jordan.

JIR – Jordanian Information Resource (2005). *Banking and Finance.* Available at: <*Url: http://reference.allrefer.com/country-guide-study/jordan/*>, Access date: 9th September, 2005.

Khamis, M. (2003). *Financial Sector Reforms and Issues in Jordan: Central Bank of Jordan.* Paper presented at the Euro-Med Regional Economic Dialogue, Rome.

Sabi, M. (1996). "Comparative Analysis of Foreign and Domestic Bank Operation in Hungary", *Journal of Comparative Economics,* 22 (2) April, pp. 179-188.

Saidi, N. (2004). "Financial Sector Development and Reform", *Economic Research Forum (ERF) Studies,* 11(2), pp. 9-13.

Saleh, A. S. and Zeitun, Rami (2005). "Development of Islamic Banking in Lebanon: Prospects and Future Challenges", *Review of Islamic Economics,* 9 (2), pp. 72-91.

Samad, A. (1999). "Comparative Efficiency of the Islamic Bank Malaysia *vis-a-vis* Conventional Banks", *HUM Journal of Economics and Management,* 7 (i), pp. 1-25.

Samad, A. and Hassan, M. K. (1999). "The Performance of Malaysian Islamic Bank During 1984-1997: An Exploratory Study", *International Journal of Islamic Financial Services,* i (3).

Sarker, A. (1999). "Islamic Banking in Bangladesh: Performance, Problems and Prospects", *International Journal of Islamic Financial Services,* i (3).

10

Funding and Financing in Islamic Banking System

Achmad Tohirin and Abdul Ghafar Ismail

***Purpose* – Aims to analyze the relation between deposit and financing sides of Islamic banking industry in Malaysia.**

***Design/methodology/approach* – The Granger causality test has been applied to examine the causality between deposit and financing.**

***Findings* – The results show that unidirectional relationship between deposit and financing exists. However, the result also shows that the directional relationship change when the test uses different lags.**

***Originality/value* – Initiate further analysis of profit-loss sharing deposits in relation to profit-loss sharing financing (mudarabah contracts) and derive its importance implications.**

Background

The last two decades we witnessed the development and progress of Islamic banking not only in Muslim countries, but also in Western countries such as Europe,

Source: www.ukm.my/ekonis.

United States and Australia. As Burghardt & Fuβ (2004) observed that today, Islamic Banking comprises a total estimated world wide volume of USD 180 billions to USD 250 billions managed by 200 to 250 financial institutions in 70 countries all over the world. They also indicated that since the year 2000, the number of Islamic Banking products has grown from approximately 40 to over 100 products with offerings particularly focusing on the fields of private banking and institutional clients.

The distinctive feature of this relatively new banking system lies on the elimination of interest rate since it is prohibited according to the Islamic Teachings. Instead, the Islamic banking scheme applies profit & loss sharing (PLS) system to operate the intermediary functions. Nik Hassan, N Mustapha, and Musa, M. (2004) highlighted that the Islamic banking system must thus seek to realize economic justice and to create an environment for economic cooperation to take place among individuals. By refusing to compartmentalize existence into secular and sacred, Islam subjects all human efforts and activities to both spiritual and rational scrutiny. The spiritualization and moralization of individual and collective economic activities of the banking system, for example, will certainly promote economic justice and cooperation. The end result of this approach would be economic efficiency, productivity, growth and stability.

The International Association of Islamic Banks (IAB) statement on the duty of Islamic banks towards the society is that the Islamic banking system involves a social implication, which is necessarily connected with the Islamic order itself, and represents a special characteristic that distinguishes Islamic banks from other banks based on other philosophies. In exercising all its banking or developmental activities, the Islamic bank takes into prime consideration the social implications that may be brought about any decision or action taken by the bank. Profitability – despite its importance and priority – is not, therefore, the sole criterion or the prime element in evaluating the performance of Islamic banks, since they have to match both between the material and the social objectives that would serve the interest of community as a whole and help achieve their role in the sphere of social mutual guarantee. Social goals are understood to form an inseparable element of the Islamic banking system that cannot be dispensed with or neglected. (IAIB, 1990).

In general, Islamic banks have two major responsibilities. One is to ensure that depositors are safe. Second is to ensure that they would be able to help achieve the

Islamic economic goals of providing social economic justice for all (no name, 2002). Though it is still relatively a new concept, Islamic banking systems have been contributing to economic development in the adopting countries through their intermediary functions. It is shown by high growth in deposits mobilization and also funds allocation to business sector. Nienhauss (1988) said that Islamic banks should provide capitals to entrepreneurs that have good projects but no collateral, and are capable of managing the project (no name 2002).

One reason for this paper to be important in looking at funding side of Islamic banking to be connected to its financing side is to look into the asset-liability management. In this regard, it is argued that Islamic banking should rely very much on its depositor's funds, beside its own equity/shareholders' funds, to be able to reward and provide a fair returns to them, in advancing its financing. In other words, Islamic banking should not utilize funding from liquidity (money) market in the first place, to extend the financing. Because it might have negative impact on optimizing the use of depositor's fund, especially in terms of returns, distribution and cost of funds. The fact that the Finance to Deposits Ratio (FDR), as shown in Table 1, tends to exceeding 100 percent might be implied that Islamic banks beside using depositors funds and their own equity capitals, it also used the funds procured from liquidity (money) market.

This paper is divided into six sections. Section One discuss the introduction, followed by Section Two to describe briefly on the Islamic concepts on financial contracts, then Section Three reveals the practices of PLS Concept under Islamic banking system, combined with Section Four to expose at a glance the facts on deposits and financing in Islamic banking. Section Five, as the main section, analyzes the causality test between deposits and financing to be closed with conclusions in Section Six.

Islamic Concepts on Financial Contracts

Islamic doctrines of contract are aimed to have effect to the society on several aspects as follows (Billah, M.M., 2006):

- Spiritual and Morality Development
- Awareness of Duties and Rights
- Establishment of Justice

- Prevention of Violence
- Inculcating the Spirit of Unity and Brotherhood
- Assurance of Security
- Economic Growth and Development

The doctrines of contract will support realization of the welfare of individual and community as well, as Islam perceived human being as individual creature and social creature at the same time.

Under Islamic concept, financial contracts can simply be categorized into two types, as follows:

1. PLS Contracts, consists of
   a. *Mudarabah* Contract (Co-partnership)
   b. *Musharakah* Contract (Partnerships)
2. Non PLS Contracts, consists of various trading contracts such as;
   a. *Murabahah* Contract (Sales)
   b. *Salam* (Purchase by Order)
   c. *Istisna.* (Manufacturing)
   d. *Ijarah* (Lease)
   e. *Wadiah* (Safe Custody)
   f. *Wakalah* (Agency)
   g. *Kafalah* (Surety), etc.

Iqbal and Llewellyn (2002) argued that the modes of financing used by Islamic banks are, however, unique for two reasons. First, debts associated with financing by way of mark-up modes results from real commodity sale/purchase operations, rather than the exchange of money for interest-bearing debt. Second, the introduction into banking of modes that depend on profit sharing is an innovation that brings important advantages. PLS contracts are the distinctive feature of Islamic Financial Institution as compared to conventional system. Under this type of contracts, each party involved would be willing to share profit and loss and also willing to share risk from conducted business ventures. This contract might be able to provide a bridge between entrepreneurs who have business skills but lack of capital and capital providers with their capital. Highly skilled entrepreneurs have the ability to entice prospective and profitable business opportunities in an economy. This important characteristic might enhance economic activities further as long as the required capital can be provided. As a result more job opportunity can be created.

In this regard, Matthews, Tlemsani and Siddiqui, (2004) highlighted that the Islamic economic principles of sharing risks and rewards, and joint participation in the wealth creation activity by borrower and lender through substituting equity for debt, is a potential solution that promotes entrepreneurship and creativity in the economic cycle. More over, they suggested that Islamic principles require equity participants actively to benchmark proposed projects against moral standards in addition to financial parameters, leading to wider community participation in the wealth creation process. In the Islamic economic model, the borrower and lender relationship is transformed into a partnership through risk sharing and in particular the sharing of profit (and loss). Choudhury (1992) argued that there is an intrinsic structure of profit sharing ratios that can be considered optimal in any *mudarabah* contract. The optimal profit sharing ratio depends upon market forces acting on the supply and demand of capital in a joint venture when it is subjected varying levels of profit shares. *Mudarabah* contracts in labor-intensive cooperatives would constitute a high proportion of equity in the form of wages foregone or the imputed value sharing in terms of labour time.

Based on those statements, it is understood that PLS contracts might drive fairness and justness for each contracting parties and might create awareness of brotherhood through partnership and cooperation among members of society. Though the impact might be very contrast compared to the contracts undertaken in conventional financial institution applying mechanism of interest rates.

Practices of PLS Concept under Islamic Banking System

Under the Islamic banking system, the fixed pricing mechanism is removed as this system applies profit and loss sharing system on both sides of the intermediary function. The removal of fixed pricing might have important implication to the performance of Islamic banking. The banks might not bear fixed cost of (investment) deposit whose volume is quite high as what happens in conventional banking system.

On Funding Side

Due to co-existence approach in many countries, Islamic banking should be able to provide similar function of deposit as in conventional banks for the sake of competition side. All types of deposits under the conventional banking system are based on the interest rates. On the funding side of Islamic banking system, the deposits will be based either on safe-custody, using *wadiah* contract, (for current account/demand deposit accounts and saving accounts) or on investment, applying *mudarabah* contract, (for saving account and time deposit accounts). These differences will also have important implication to some aspects of the risks management of the Islamic banks. Under the safe custody and investment-based models, the deposited funds will not create fixed burden, measured by cost, for the banks as in the conventional interest-based banks do. In this regard though, the cost of funds, for the banks will possibly be lower than the same cost under the conventional banking system. It might become a positive advantage for achieving the banks' cost efficiency. Even though, it might also create a kind of less incentive to optimize the use of funds by the banks, market mechanism (discipline) might enhance it. Bashir (1983), concluded that the cost of funds to current accounts are represented by foregone profitable investments, while the cost of attracting funds to deposit accounts are caused by the increase in the number of participators in the banks profits. This unique decision policy results from the participatory finance method of Islamic banks, and the supply functions of funds which are here assumed to be affected by the decision policy.

Hassoune (2002) argued that, Islamic banks do not share their "profits" with depositors, because profit is defined as the final amount of wealth attributable to shareholders in a period of time. What is shared between shareholders and depositors is a variable one can define as the bank's "Income Before Cost Funding" (IBCF), equities being excluded here from the scope of funding. The cost of non-equity funds is precisely what distinguishes Islamic banks from conventional banks. While conventional banks rely on debt and deposits with mainly fixed interest rates, Islamic banks rely on a funding base whose cost depends on the return of its assets. In mobilizing funds from the customers, the Islamic banks offer safe-custody based products, reflected in the Current Accounts and the Saving Accounts and investment based deposits, reflected in the Saving Account and the Time Deposits Accounts.

Under the Islamic banking system, the depositors will only be offered a profit sharing ratio by the Islamic banks, for example 60:40. This ratio indicates the proportion of profit that will go to the depositors (60 percent) and the banks (40 percent). It does not reveal explicitly either the rate of return for the depositor or the cost of funds for the banks. How much 60 percent worth for the depositors or 40 percent for the banks is uncertain. It will depend on the banks' profitability performance. The equivalent rates of return can only be provided for the previous periods of time and it is not invariant due to the banks performance measured by their profitability. This is the most important difference between Islamic banks and conventional banks. Since the return or portion of profit given to the depositors will follow the banks profitability measure, the fixed cost (of funds) character is no longer burdening the banks as what happens in the conventional banks. In this respect, the fairness is more obvious, due to the prevailing equitable distribution of risk between the banks and the depositors (Tohirin, 2004).

By nature, Islamic banking is a banking system oriented toward equity (equity based system). Mohsin S. Khan (1992) stated that the Islamic Banking System is an equity-based system in which depositors are treated as if they were shareholders of a bank. Consequently, deposits are not guaranteed the nominal value of their deposits or a predetermined rate of return on these deposits. If the bank makes profits then the shareholder (depositor) would be entitled to receive a certain proportion of these profits. On the other hand, if the bank incurs losses the depositor is expected to share in these as well, and would receive a negative rate of return. Thus, from the depositor's perspective, an Islamic Bank is in most respect identical to a mutual fund or investment trust.

On Financing Side

Lewis and Algaoud (2001) emphasized five religious features that must be followed in investment behaviour, namely;

1. The absence of interest based (*riba*) financial transactions;
2. The introduction of a religious levy or almsgiving, *zakat*;
3. The prohibition of production of goods and services which contradict the value pattern of Islam, (*haram*);

4. The avoidance of economic activities involving *maysir* (gambling) and *gharar* (uncertainty);
5. The provision of *takaful* (Islamic insurance)

Following Khalil, Rickwood, and Murinde (2002), from the bank perspective, there are three distinctive features of *mudarabah* contract. The first is the idiosyncratic uncertainty (risk), e.g. the bank's return is assumed to solely depend on the reported future cash flows resulted from operating profitability, which in turn depends entirely on the corporate investment decisions that are made by the agent. The second is the extreme linearity (linear-sharing) between the reward and the performance of the project undertaken, where the party's reward is a linear function of the realized income. The third is the discretionary power since the agent initially controls the project and enjoys the rights to make decisions concerning investment and distribution of intermediate cash flows.

Khalil, Rickwood, and Murinde (2002) identified that there are two main reasons that prevent bank from entering into *mudarabah* contract, namely misreporting of the result of the project and the uncertainty and variability of the return from *mudarabah* contract. Misreporting relates to moral hazard problem from the side of entrepreneur financed by the bank to mark-up the cost to have less profit to be distributed between them. Due to this potential problem attached to *mudarabah* contract, it implies that there has to be mechanism to prevent this problem through appropriate monitoring system. As for the problem of uncertainty and variability of *mudarabah* contract's return, it is the nature of this contract which directs the result of contract to depend upon the performance of the project to follow the business cycles.

Islamic banking allocates their funds, sourcing mainly from customers' deposits and their shareholder's fund as their paid-up capital, into financing theirs client's projects and investing into money market and capital market securities. In this respect, the ratio of financing to deposit might provide important information on the effectiveness of intermediary function of banks. The higher the ratio of financing to deposit, means the more effective the bank in performing intermediary function. On the contrary, the lesser the ratio means the less effective the bank in performing intermediary function. The effectiveness of banking intermediary function might have significant impact on the macroeconomic performance, such as the levels of output, price, employment, and so on.

Figure 1: Financing Techniques in Islamic Banking

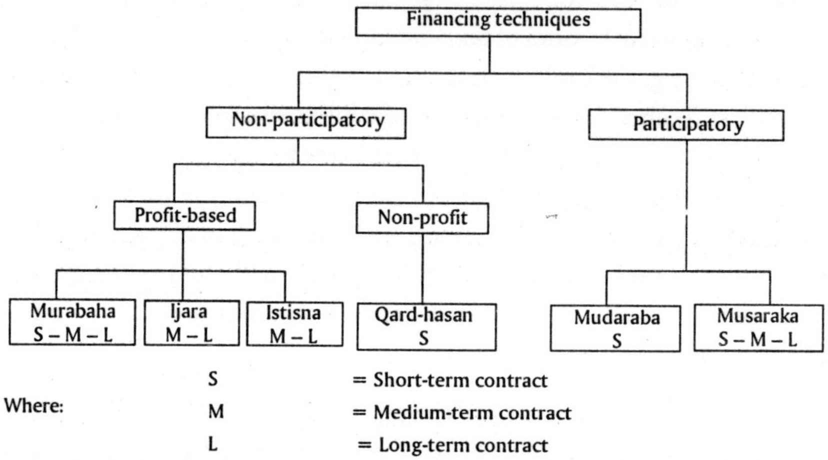

Source: Burghardt, and Fuâ (2004)

The Facts on Deposits and Financing in Islamic Banking

Looking at the data on deposits in Table 1, it shows how the structure of deposits looks like. The total deposits consist of:

- Demand Deposits
- Saving Deposits
- Investment Deposits

Investment deposit dominates other types of deposits, ranging from 64 to 74 percent of total deposits. This type of deposits uses *mudarabah* contract. The structure might not significantly different from that in conventional banking system, as it is one mode of investing fund available in financial industry. However, further look need to be done on the diminishing trend of investment deposit in Islamic banking industry in Malaysia. As for Demand and Saving Deposits, both shares range from 16 to 22 percent and 10 to 14 percent respectively with increasing trends.

On the other part of Table 1, financing types are exhibited. The total financing comprises four types of financing namely;

- Overdraft
- Term Financing
- Bill Financing
- Other Financing

It is unfortunate that due to this type of financing classifications, it is difficult to compare the *mudarabah* contracts on financing side to those in deposits side to see the balance. However, due to various problems arising from implementing *mudarabah* contract in financing, Islamic banking system tends to channel its financing by relying very much on *murabahah* or *bai' bithaman 'ajil* contracts and other non-PLS financing. As in Table 1, Term Financing is very dominant to other types of financing. It counts 79 to 82 percent during the period of Quarter 1 of 2002 to Quarter 1 of 2004. This structure of financing is common practices for Islamic banking companies around the world.

Table 1: Percentage of Deposits and Financing of Islamic Banking in Malaysia

Date	Deposit Types			Financing Types				Finance to Deposit Ratio
	Demand Deposit	Investment Deposit	Saving Deposit	Over Draft	Term Financing	Bill Financing	Other Financing	
Q1'02	16.73	73.55	9.71	2.20	81.73	6.75	9.31	6.26
Q2	16.01	73.55	10.44	2.26	80.41	6.62	0.72	0.80
Q3	16.40	72.93	10.68	2.18	79.51	6.82	1.49	5.34
Q4	18.24	70.54	11.23	2.25	79.08	7.55	11.12	9.07
Q1'03	19.41	68.52	12.07	2.63	79.34	6.68	11.35	83.80
Q2	18.60	69.07	12.33	2.74	80.39	6.28	10.59	87.17
Q3	19.82	67.14	13.04	2.60	82.15	5.71	9.55	95.43
Q4	21.46	64.90	13.64	2.64	82.03	5.95	9.38	98.97
Q1'04	21.86	63.73	14.41	2.80	81.79	6.24	9.17	100.89

Source: Annual Reports of Bank Negara Malaysia (various numbers)

Table 1 also displays Finance to Deposit Ratio (FDR). This ratio suggested that the intermediary function of Islamic banking works properly, as most of fund mobilized through deposits can be allocated into financing. It may also be inferred that the Islamic banking is capable of supporting the real sector of the economy in driving more economic and productive activities. This might be positively considered as closing the gap between banking sector and real sector and might contribute to improving supply sides of the economy and its stabilization efforts. As we know that for a bank, allocation of mobilized funds might take several forms other than financing, such as investing in securities in money market or central bank certificates, etc.

Causality Test between Deposits and Financing

In this section, further analysis on deposit and financing in Islamic banking system will be conducted by mean of Granger's Causality Test. To that end, monthly data for total deposits and total financing in Islamic Banking of Malaysia from January 2001 to May 2004 will be used. It covers 41 months period.

As a standard procedure before performing causality test, it is necessary to conduct unit root test to check the stationarity of the series. Figure 2 and Figure 3 displays the series of total deposits and total financing at their levels (DEP and FIN) and at their first differenced D(FINDEP) and D(FINFIN) respectively. Figure 2 indicates positive trend for both series, i.e. it incorporates growth in bothseries.

Figure 2: Islamic Bank Deposits and Financing (at Level)

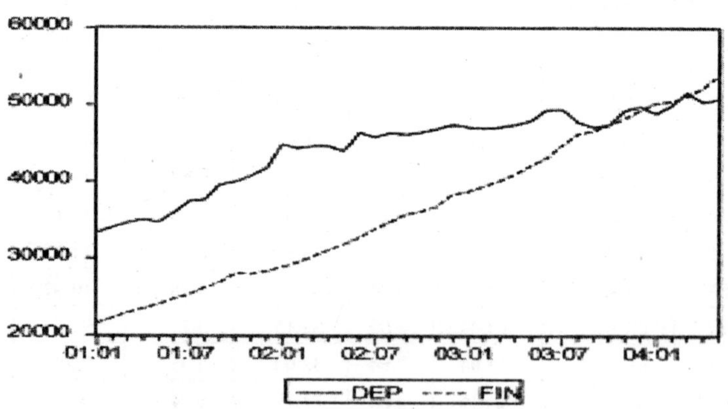

To carry out unit root test, the Augmented Dickey Fuller (ADF) test has been applied through the following equation (Gujarati, 2003):

$$\Delta Y_t = \beta_1 + \beta_2 t + \delta Y_{t-1} + \alpha_1 \Sigma^{m}{}_{t=1} + \Delta Y_{t-i} + \varepsilon_t \quad (1)$$

Figure 3: Islamic Bank Deposits and Financing (at First Differenced)

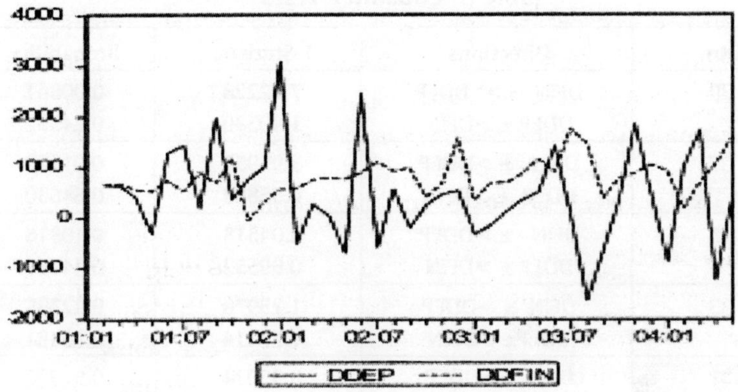

Table 2 exhibits the results of the ADF unit root test for the first-differenced series of Deposits and Financing. The results show that the first-differenced series are already stationary and hence these series will be used to conduct the Granger causality test.

Table 2: Unit Root Tests

Method			Statistic	Prob.**
ADF – Fisher Chi-square			44.7213	0.0000
ADF - Choi Z-stat			-5.90399	0.0000
Intermediate ADF test results				
Series	**Prob.**	**Lag**	**Max Lag**	**Obs**
D(FINDEP)	0.0000	0	9	38
D(FINFIN)	0.0001	0	9	38

Source: Computed Data

After conducting ADF unit root test, then the Granger causality test can be implemented by estimating the following two equations:

$$\Delta FINFIN_t = \Sigma^n{}_{i=1} \alpha_i \Delta FINFIN_{t-i} + \alpha_i \Sigma^m{}_{j=1} \beta_j \Delta FINDEP_{t-i} + \mu_{1t} \tag{2}$$

$$\Delta FINFIN_t = \Sigma^n{}_{i=1} \alpha_i \Delta FINDEP_{t-i} + \alpha_i \Sigma^m{}_{j=1} \beta_j \Delta FINFIN_{t-i} + \mu_{2t} \tag{3}$$

The results of Granger causality test are exhibited in Table 3.

Table 3: Causality Tests

Lags	Obs.	Directions	F-Statistic	Probability
1	39	DFIN ±>* DDEP	7.72228	0.00861
		DDEP ± >DFIN	1.40580	0.24352
3	37	DFIN ± >DDEP	3.95952	0.01720
		DDEP ± >DFIN	0.55885	0.64630
5	35	DFIN ± >DDEP	2.04518	0.10816
		DDEP ± >DFIN	0.99532	0.44151
7	33	DFIN ± >DDEP	1.25970	0.32355
		DDEP± >DFIN	1.77314	0.15481
9	31	DFIN ±>DDEP	0.95014	0.51990
		DDEP ± >DFIN	3.17695	0.03283
11	29	DFIN ±>DDEP	0.46166	0.87362
		DDEP ± >DFIN	3.03350	0.09244

* : does not Granger cause

Source: Computed Data

The results show different results under different number of lags used in the test. Initially, at lag 1 the null hypothesis that DFIN does not Granger cause DDEP, is rejected, where as, the null hypothesis that DDEP does not Granger cause DFIN is accepted. It is meant that unidirectional relationship exists between DFIN and DDEP. The same pattern is resulted when lag 3 is used. Very different result can be seen when lag 9 is used. It accepts the null hypothesis that DFIN does not Granger cause DDEP. However, the null hypothesis that DDEP does not Granger cause DFIN is rejected. This is the result that is expected, based on the theoretical background. As it is known that for banks, financing will only be available if they have enough funds mobilized through deposits. It can be established that the availability of deposits that will enable banks to provide financing to their investor customers. The result from causality test, however, is in line with this proposition.

Conclusion

In discussing relation between deposits and financing in Islamic bank, this paper has been able to prove the unidirectional causal relationship, meaning that deposits mobilized by banks that will enable banks to provide financing to their investment customers. However, this paper is unable to explore more information concerning the causality relationship especially for *mudarabah* deposit and *mudarabah* financing due to the unavailability of the data with the required classification.

(Achmad Tohirin, Center for Islamic Economics Development and Studies (CIEDS), Faculty of Economics, Universitas Islam Indonesia, Yogyakarta, Indonesia. The author can be reached at ahmad@fe.uii.ac.id.

Abdul Ghafar Ismail, Islamic Economics and Finance Research Group School of Economics, Universiti Kebangsaan Malaysia, Selangor, Malaysia. The author can be reached at my agibab1986@yahoo.co.uk).

References

Bashir, B.A. (1983), "Portfolio management of Islamic banks 'certainty model'", *Journal of Banking and Finance*, Vol. 7, No.3, pp. 339-54.

Billah, M.M. (2006), *Shariah Standard of Business Contract*, A.S.Noordeen, Kuala Lumpur.

Burghardt, I., and Fu β, C. (2004), "Islamic banking credit products in Germany and in the UK", working paper series No. 12, Dept. of Finance, European Business School, International University Schlo β Reichartshausen.

Choudhury, M.A. (1992), *The Principles of Islamic Political Economy, A Methodological Enquiry*, St Martin's Press, New York.

Gujarati, D.N. (2003), *Basic Econometrics*, 4th edition, Mc-Graw Hill.

Hassoune, A. (2002), "Islamic banks' profitability in an interest rate cycle", *International Journal of Islamic Financial Services*, Vol. 4, No. 2, pp. 1-13.

Iqbal, M., and Llewellyn, D.T. (2002), "Introduction", *Islamic Banking and Finance, New Perspectives on Profit-Sharing and Risk.* Edward Elgar, Cheltenham, UK, Northhampton, MA, USA.

Kaleem, A., and Isa, M. Md., (2002), "Causal relationship between Islamic and conventional banking instruments in Malaysia", *International Journal of Islamic Financial Services*, Vol.4, No. 4, pp. 1-8.

Khalil, A.F.A.A., Rickwood, C. and Murinde, V. (2002). "Evidence on agency-contractual problems in mudarabah financing operation by Islamic banks", In Iqbal, M. and Llewellyn, D.T. *Islamic Banking and Finance, New Perspectives on Profit-Sharing and Risk.* Edward Elgar, Cheltenham, UK, Northhampton, MA, USA.

Lewis, M.K., and Algaoud, L.M. (2001), *Islamic Banking,* Edward Elgar, Cheltenham, UK, Northhampton, MA, USA.

Matthews, R., Tlemsani, I., and Siddiqui, A. (2004), "Islamic banking and the mortgage market in the UK", in Shanmugam, Bala. *et al.* (2004), *Islamic Banking: An International Perspective,* Universiti Putra Malaysia Press, Serdang, Malaysia.

Nik Hassan, N Mustapha, and Musa, M. (2004), "An evaluation of Islamic Banking Development in Malaysia", in Shanmugam, Bala *et al.* (2004), *Islamic Banking: An International Perspective,*Universiti Putra Malaysia Press, Serdang, Malaysia.

No name, 2002, "Issues in Islamic banking profit and loss sharing as a mode of Islamic financing", unpublished draft paper from *www.scirus.com/profitsharing.*

Tohirin, Achmad. (2004), "Mudharabah contracts: comparing depositors and shareholders in Islamic banking system, *Proceedings of National Seminar on Islamic Banking,* Islamic University College of Malaysia, pp. 279-88.

11

Risk Management: Islamic Financial Policies – Islamic Banking and its Potential Impact*

Thomas A Timberg

Islamic instruments are simply a narrow group of familiar financing instruments. Any transaction, with any distribution of proceeds, can be conducted as a lease, a sale, a partnership, a fee-generating transaction, or a loan. Islamic instruments generally avoid loans. Though the scheduled distribution of proceeds may be the same as for a conventional loan, the legal risk in case of default is often different in the different forms of financing. Indonesia, with the world's largest population of Muslims, has come to Islamic or shariah banking fairly late. Many of Indonesia's Muslim leaders do not believe that commercial interest in its modern form is prohibited, although others do. After some false starts, Islamic financial institutions

* This case study was made possible by the support provided in part by the US Agency for International Development (USAID) Agreement No. LAG-A-00-96-90016-00 through Broadening Access and Strengthening Input Market Systems Collaborative Research Support Program (BASIS-CRSP) and the World Council of Credit Unions, Inc. (WOCCU).

Source: www.basis.wisc.edu © Thomas A Timberg. This paper was originally presented at "Paving the Way Forward for Rural Finance: An International Conference on Best Practices", June 2-4, 2003. Reprinted with permission.

are developing rapidly and have the enthusiastic support of many young people and intellectuals. The work of the Shariah Bureau of Bank Indonesia demonstrates that Indonesia, especially in particular parts of the country, has considerable unmet demand for Islamic banking.

Islamic Banking and its Potential Impact

This is a little different from other case studies being presented at this conference. Since the representatives of the Shariah Bureau of Bank Indonesia responsible for the supervision and development of Islamic finance will focus on the experience and progress of Islamic banking in Indonesia, I will focus on some questions about the impacts of that banking, particularly in rural areas, and aspects that the Bank Indonesia representatives will not focus on.

Islamic banking is a worldwide phenomenon involving a variety of institutions and instruments, not one "project" or institution. In the past few decades, Islamic institutions and instruments have developed in many countries, including the United States. In certain countries—Iran, Sudan, and Pakistan—all or most financial intermediation conforms to Islamic shariah (religious law) as defined by local authorities. All three of these countries also have banking authorities that govern the general level of charges and returns in the system and these are not usually market-governed systems.

In most other countries, including Indonesia, Islamic transactions and institutions make up a small part of the total and must compete with conventional financial institutions. There is even considerable Islamic banking in the United States.[1] If the terms and conditions of Islamic transactions differ too much from those of conventional institutions they become hard to sustain. The terms and conditions of Islamic institutions, therefore, tend to converge with conventional ones.[2]

Islamic instruments are simply a narrow group of familiar financing instruments. Any transaction, with any distribution of proceeds, can be conducted as a lease, a sale, a partnership, a fee-generating transaction, or a loan. Islamic instruments generally avoid loans. Though the scheduled distribution of proceeds may be the same as for a conventional loan, the legal risk in case of default is often different in the different forms of financing.

Those who promote Islamic finance often prefer partnership arrangements in which profits or turnover is shared because this conforms more fully to the goals of Islamic banking.[3] One goal of Bank Indonesia in promoting Islamic banking is to increase the proportion of financing involving such sharing.[4] Nonetheless, more than 80 percent of Indonesian Islamic financing is in fixed-term forms, mirroring the pattern throughout the world.[5]

Many involved in Islamic banking would like to minimize the differences between Islamic and conventional banking and thus they welcome fixed-term forms. However, because the instruments differ in some degree they typically require some adjustment from their conventional counterparts.[6] For example, in Islamic transactions, the bank often holds the title of the property concerned. US banking authorities have ruled this unobjectionable provided that title holding is only a matter of form to accommodate Islamic strictures.[7]

Although US and other banking supervision authorities have accommodated Islamic banking with few changes in procedures, some countries consider that this is not enough. They have moved to develop national and international Islamic institutions—money markets, bank regulators, deposit protection, bank accounting, and so on. Centers have been developed for all these matters—for bank supervision in Malaysia, for accounting in Bahrain, and several academic centers, including centers at Harvard and Oxford universities.[8]

The Example of Indonesia

Indonesia, with the world's largest population of Muslims, has come to Islamic or shariah banking fairly late. Many of Indonesia's Muslim leaders do not believe that commercial interest in its modern form is prohibited, although others do. After some false starts, Islamic financial institutions are developing rapidly and have the enthusiastic support of many young people and intellectuals. The work of the Shariah Bureau of Bank Indonesia demonstrates that Indonesia, especially in particular parts of the country, has considerable unmet demand for Islamic banking.[9]

Islamic banking in Indonesia has some unusual characteristics. Like most microfinance institutions in Indonesia, Islamic institutions, micro or otherwise, are generally private, for-profit institutions based on the intermediation of depositor funds secured on a competitive market. In this, they are different from microfinance institutions in almost every other country in the world. They typically have no explicit social goal other than profit maximization and conformity with Islam, though in some cases a social element is present, as we will see. Social impacts are thus the result of the market impacts of the Islamic institutions.

Many Islamic institutions in Indonesia, particularly the Bait Maal Wat Tamwil (BMT)—Islamic savings and loan cooperatives—are located in rural areas and provide agricultural financing. Nonetheless, the focus of Indonesian Islamic financial institutions is typically urban and geared toward the financing of trading operations. There has been some discussion of Islamic banking for microcredit, but most documented experience that I know of is in Pakistan, where institutions charge a service fee to cover their costs— something that is not permitted now in many Islamic banking systems.

In terms of agricultural finance, I have encountered only one institution, a BMT in Solo, that provided crop loans. This transaction, which involved a fixed repayment in kind, also might not meet the standards of many Islamic lenders. I am sure other crop loans exist. A couple of Islamic financial instruments are particularly—and according to one source, traditionally—designed for agriculture.

The lending of the various venture capital firms in Indonesia, the Modal Ventura, did support a number of agribusiness ventures on an Islamic, profit-sharing basis. The example is not necessarily an attractive one, however, because although repayment was frequently high, the profit-sharing element, in which low profits were reported, and the devaluation of the Indonesian rupiah led to the decapitalization of these venture capital firms.

Islamic financial institutions in Indonesia include the Bank Muamalat Indonesia, which has been functioning since 1992, several new Islamic branches of regular commercial banks, one other newer commercial bank, 80 Bank Perkreditan Rakyat Shariah (BPRS—smaller banks limited to borrowing and lending in limited areas), and 2,470 BMT (of which a few are reported to be registered with the Ministry of Cooperatives and Small Business). The Islamic commercial banks and BPRS file frequent and detailed reports with Bank Indonesia and thus produce reliable and current statistics. This is not yet the case with BMT.[10]

The amount of funds in Islamic institutions has been growing rapidly, as the paper, "The Blueprint of Islamic Banking in Indonesia," which is also being presented at this session, illustrates. Assets in Islamic banks have grown from US$52 million to US$302 million but still account for only 0.26 percent of assets in the banking system. The figure is somewhat higher if we exclude the considerable assets of conventional banks that represent government recapitalization bonds of one sort or another. Bank Indonesia has been moving to ensure that support institutions are developed for Islamic banks.[11]

I will present some data on the largest and oldest Islamic bank, Bank Muamalat, and the BMT because they will not be presented elsewhere at this conference.

Bank Muamalat

Bank Muamalat's position as of December 31, 2002 (from quarterly reports posted on the Bank Indonesia website) can be seen in the following Table.[12] Various small approximations were made; precise concepts are specified in Bank Indonesia sources.

Bank	Assets	Credit	Deposits	Nonperforming Loans (%)
Bank Muamalat	238	190	190	4.8
Bank Mandiri	28,103	7,101	20,444	6.6
Banking System	123,556	45,556	92,778	8.1

Bank Muamalat's loans, according to its recent annual audited reports, are distributed among Islamic financial instruments as shown in Table 1. (Definitions for these instruments are given in the Appendix.)

About two-thirds of the rupiah financing and half of the foreign currency financing are for less than one year. This is a high level of longer-term financing for a commercial bank. There is a trend toward mudharabah. The average return on loans seems to be a little more than 10 percent, which is not high by Indonesian standards.

Bank Muamalat splits gross revenues with borrowers, not net profit as in other Islamic institutions, and almost always insists on collateral. Its "sharing," non-fixed term lending is thus easier for it to manage than it would be in some other countries.

Table 1: Bank Muamalat Loans by Type of Shariah Instrument (Rp billion)		
Financing Instrument	**1998**	**1997**
For Rupiah		
Bai Bitsaman Ajil	141	179
Murabahah	83	130
Mudharabah	68	29
Musyarakah	13	12
Al Qardhul Hasan	1	1
Total	**306**	**351**
For Foreign Currencies		
Bai Bitsaman Ajil	78	86
Murabahah	71	21
Mudarabah	7	1
Total	**156**	**108**
Grand Total	**462**	**459**

The bank made a profit when many Indonesian banks were losing money. It used to have a higher percentage of nonperforming loans, but the situation appears to be improving. The pattern of outside funds deposited in Bank Muamalat by instrument can be seen in the following figures, from a similar source to Table 2.

Savings and Returns	1998 Amount	1998 Returns
Mudharabah Time Deposits	221	28
Securities	***	23
Mudarabah Savings Deposits	103	7
Wadiah Demand Deposits	68	3
Others		3

The cost of outside funds seems to be roughly half that charged borrowers—again somewhat low by Indonesian standards. Bank Muamalat reports that despite its relatively low payment of 10-12 percent on deposits, while other banks were paying in the mid-20s, the nominal amount of deposits declined by only 15 percent. This reflects the strong customer loyalty enjoyed by all Islamic financial institutions. In recent months a number of banks have opened or announced that they will shift to Islamic principles or open shariah branches, so competition for Bank Muamalat is likely to increase.

Bank Muamalat has a specifically social focus, as noted in its 1998 annual report. Its mission is "to become the catalyst for Islamic financial institution development," and "enhance its role in small scale industry finance." Almost 17 percent of its lending goes to small and medium enterprises, which is above average for commercial banks. Bank Muamalat intends to "selectively [distribute] its financing with emphasis on small businesses by using its shariah financial institution network," 29 of the 78 BPRS, and 100 of the 2,000 BMT, and aspires, as well, to serve the kopontren (registered multipurpose cooperatives connected with pesantren, Islamic school dormitories), which often have a savings and credit unit.

Bank Muamalat is also one of three sponsors that conduct extensive training for BMT. The other training sponsors are the Indonesian Council of Muslim Intellectuals and the Majlis Ulema Indonesia (a group of Islamic scholars) of Yayasan Inkubasi Bisnis Usaha Kecil (Foundation for Incubating Small Businesses (YINBUK).

Bank Perkreditan Rakyat Shariah

The roughly 80 shariah BPRS have Rp 80.5 billion in total assets. They were created as a legal category under the 1988 banking reforms. They are permitted to borrow and lend money but do not have access to the payments system, have lower capital requirements than commercial banks, and are subject to inspection by Bank Indonesia. BPRS have been growing rapidly (as noted in the Bank Indonesia Blueprint) although they still constitute a small portion of the total.

Bait Maal Wat Tamwil—Islamic Savings and Loan Cooperatives

The BMT savings and loan cooperatives follow Islamic procedures as well. So far only a few of these are registered with the Ministry of Cooperation and Small Enterprise and are subject to its rules. The BMT, like the BPRS, more or less follow the general rules for savings and loan co-ops.

Most BMT are associated with Induk Koperasi Syariah BMT (Inkopsyah BMT), which was established by 18 registered Islamic BMT and 2,200 unregistered "pre–coops."[13] Other BMT are associated with other organizations, especially the foundation Dompet Dhuafa and some religious organizations, or are independent.

The registered cooperatives are either free-standing savings and loan cooperatives (Koperasi Simpan Pinjam–KSP) or units in broader cooperatives (Unit Simpan Pinjam—USP). I visited one Islamic USP that was part of a multipurpose cooperative that operated a store and garment factory as well as the USP; another was part of a kopontren. BMT, even free-standing ones, typically are closely associated with other Islamic institutions.The Mohamadiya Polyteknik in Karaganyar told us that it has five BMT associated with it.

The legal status of BMT, unless they are registered as cooperatives, is ambiguous, although the Ministry of Cooperatives and local governments often work with them. Pusat Inkubasi Bisnis Usaha Kecil (Center for Incubating Small Businesses [PINBUK]) has helped develop a regulatory system for them, and USAID contributed to a national seminar on the subject. A strong consensus exists on the need for some regulatory scheme to be developed, but the form that such a scheme would take is still unclear.

As of June 1998, there were 330,000 members in 2,470 BMT with Rp 187 billion in outstanding loans in this network. The number of BMT rose from 300 at the end of 1995 to 700 at the end of 1996 and 1,501 at the end of 1997. The BMT currently have 8,253 paid staff, mostly university graduates, who have been trained by PINBUK. As of June 1998, of the $20 million of outstanding BMT loans, the overwhelming amount was short term, averaged $100 per loan, and went to microenterprises. About half of the borrowers are reported to be "microenterprise groups." Some of these are possibly guarantee groups of individual microentrepreneurs, but most are presumably classic NGO group enterprises. The borrowers are predominantly small traders.[14]

This $20 million of small lending was 83 percent funded by the savings of members, and 14 percent from the capital of the cooperatives. Apparently, no funds came from BPRS, though some funds have come from Bank Negara Indonesia, a government bank, Bank Maumalat, and some government enterprises, especially Pertamina. The BMT appear to be 100 percent lent up, with no liquid funds in bank accounts or cash. So far, overdue amounts are negligible; less than one-third of amounts due are more than a month overdue.[15]

Kopontren—Cooperatives Connected with Pesantren

The 1,500 kopontren connected with pesantren are registered with the Ministry of Cooperatives. Most of their savings units do not follow the Islamic system, although some are beginning to do so. One hundred to 300 of the kopontren savings units are estimated to have shifted to Islamic banking. The Islamic financial institutions look on them as an important target market segment, but much of the kopontren leadership does not want to identify solely with Islamic financial institutions. Because the pesantren are mostly in rural areas, their cooperatives and credit are frequently connected with agriculture.

Findings and Recommendations

Though Bank Muamalat and the BPRS offer a full range of Islamic deposit and credit products, most Islamic credit in Indonesia has taken the form of trade finance (bai al salaam, bai bitsama ajil, istishna, or murabaha), though the proportion declines as the partnership or trust provision of working capital (musyarakat and mudharabah) increases. Rates (charged and paid) differ considerably between institutions and from time to time, but the average rates on Islamic credit often approximate those of other institutions.

Although Bank Muamalat did not suffer as severely as many large banks from the financial crisis, it did require some management change and has begun healthy growth again. BPRS and BMT have been growing despite the monetary crisis.

The BMT have mobilized a great deal of savings and provided financial services to a large constituency, many of whom have never been served before. They have a large prospective market and the advantage of building on the informal network created by the Islamic institutions with which they are associated as well as the moral sanction that comes with that affiliation. However, as largely unsupervised and unguaranteed institutions, many of which are run by relatively inexperienced personnel using new methodologies, they clearly present prudential dangers—though not different in principle from those posed by all savings and loan cooperatives in Indonesia.

In form rather than substance, Islamic finance is familiar. Many of its instruments are the same as those used by other financial institutions—leasing, advance purchase, etc. The difference lies in the first instance in the social impulse for sharing—responsibility, risk, and property. Consequently, fixed-interest transactions in which risk is assigned entirely to the borrower are avoided. More important for participants, Islamic finance represents part of a divinely sanctioned economic gestalt into which they fit.

Thus Islamic finance:

- Enables financial services to an otherwise underserved group including small, rural, and agricultural producers;
- Furthers a social thrust to assist smaller producers and consumers and is often given in the context of a movement to assist them; but
- Requires some adjustment, mostly formal, of techniques and regulation to take account of Islamic values.

Islamic finance, as part of a financial sector development strategy, ought to be encouraged, mainstreamed, and adjusted to. An IMF study on the matter concludes that Islamic finance should be encouraged by regulation and supervision that accommodate its forms while ensuring that their unfamiliarity is not exploited to defraud clients. Normal prudential and supervision norms should be adequate. The IMF study does, however, suggest that higher capital adequacy ratios and more detailed disclosure requirements may be appropriate.[16] The paper suggests a modified CAMEL (capital adequacy, asset quality, management, earnings, liquidity) system of banking supervision for Islamic banking. Special risks are the generally uncollateralized nature of Islamic banking and greater risks in the profit-sharing forms of lending. To the extent that Islamic banking is collateralized or does not engage in profit-sharing forms, the issues are less serious. Nonetheless, the Islamic banks are often more comfortable with specialized regulations and infrastructure that recognize their peculiarities. The BMT in particular need adequate supervision and some guarantee for their depositors, though not as elaborate as those provided commercial banks and BPRs.

Islamic banking should be mainstreamed by maximizing the interaction between Islamic institutions and the rest of the financial system, subject to the constraints of shariah. The financial system and its regulation should be adjusted as necessary to accommodate the other two thrusts.

Donors should ensure that their assistance to financial system development includes Islamic financial institutions. This will help include otherwise excluded groups and avoid regulatory loopholes.

(Thomas A Timberg can be reached at ttimberg@nathaninc.com).

APPENDIX

Islamic Lending and Borrowing Instruments in Indonesia

These definitions for the borrowing and lending instruments used by Bank Muamalat, Indonesia's first shariah commercial bank. come from its 1998 annual report.[17]

Lending Forms

Advance Purchase Forms

Cost Plus Financing—Murabaha

A sales contract between the bank and the customer for the sale of goods at a price that includes a profit margin agreed to by both parties. As a financing technique it involves the purchase of goods by the bank as requested by the customer. Repayment is conducted by installments within a specified period.

Purchase with Specification—Istishna

A sales contract between the bank and the customer wherein the customer specifies goods to be made. After the goods are made or shipped the bank sells them to the customer according to a pre-agreed arrangement.

Purchase with Deferred Delivery—Bai al Salam

A sales contract whereby the price is paid in advance by the bank and the goods delivered later by the customer to a designee.

Lease and Hire Purchase—Ijarah Mutahia Bittamlik

A contract under which the bank leases equipment to a customer for a rental fee. At the end of the lease period the customer buys the equipment at an agreed price from the bank, with the rental fees already paid being part of the price.

Profit-Sharing Forms

Trust Financing/Trustee Profit-sharing—Mudharabah/Mudharabah Muqayyadah

The bank provides the capital (shahibul maal) and the customer manages the project (mudharib). The gross revenues from the project are split according to a pre-agreed ratio.

Partnership/Participation Financing—Musyarakah

A partnership between the bank customer in which profits are shared on a pre-agreed basis but losses are shared on the basis of equity contribution. This partnership may be managed by the bank or the customer, jointly, or by a third party.

Benevolent Loan—Qardh ul Hasan

An interest-free loan, generally with a charitable motivation.

Collateral Agreement—Rahn

An agreement to provide collateral to the bank, either in the bank's or the customer's custody as appropriate. This is connected with some other form of lending.

Agency/Trust—Wakalah

An agreement to authorize another to be an agent to conduct some business. In this case, an authorization to the bank to conduct some business on the customer's behalf.

Agency—Havalah

An agreement by the bank to undertake some of the liabilities of the customer. When the liabilities mature the customer pays back the bank. The bank is paid a fee for undertaking the liabilities concerned.

Borrowing Forms

Ummat Savings—Tabungan Ummat

A savings account from which money can be withdrawn any time at any Muamalat office or ATM. Customers share in the bank's revenue. The Ummat Savings customers also receive life insurance and the opportunity to win a free Umrah pilgrimage to Mecca.

Trendi Savings—Tabungan Trendi

A savings account for teenagers and students. Besides accident insurance coverage, it offers special prizes for highly ranked students and one-year scholarships for 50 students.

Ukhuwah Savings—Tabungan Ukhuwah

A savings account conducted in cooperation with Dompet Dhuafa Republika for convenience in making regular and automatic payment of zakat, infaq, and shadaqat in three packages: Rp 25,000, Rp 50,000, and Rp 100,000. This savings account also gives the depositor an ATM card, shopping discounts at certain shops, and accident insurance coverage.

Arafah Savings—Tabungan Arafah

A savings account designed specifically for the hajj pilgrimage. The saving scheme will help customers in planning their hajj in accordance with their financial capability and intended hajj date. Life insurance is also provided. The depositors are also eligible for prizes.

Fulinves Deposits—Deposito Fulinves

A time deposit with a revenue sharing package available for various terms and with a chance to win prizes. Life insurance is provided to those with longer-term deposits.

Wadi'ah Current Account—Giro Wadi'ah

A current account providing checking and allowing some profit sharing. Muamalat Financial Institution Pension Fund—Dana Pensiun Lembaga Keuangan A pension fund for those who make regular deposits. The bank intends to add a variant that provides life insurance.

Endnotes

1 See Financial Times, March 25, 2003, inter alia.

2 This fact sometimes disturbs observers who feel that they are being confronted simply with a change of nomenclature. A very articulate answer to this complaint is contained in Mahmoud Amin El-Gamal, A Basic Guide to Contemporary Islamic Banking and Finance, June 2000, at *http://www.ruf.rice.edu/~elgamal/files/primer.pdf.*

3 Zamir Iqbal, "Islamic Financial Systems," Finance and Development, June 1997, lists six basic principles: Avoidance of interest, risk sharing, treating of money as potential capital, prohibition ofspeculation, sanctity of contracts, and avoidance of prohibited activities such as those connected with alcohol and gambling. Others might disagree.

4 The word shariah rather than Islamic is usually used in Indonesia.

5 V Sundararajan and Luca Errico, Islamic Financial Institutions and Products in the Global Financial System: Key Issues in Risk Management and Challenges Ahead, IMF Working Paper No. WP/02/192, Washington, D.C.: IMF, 2002, at *http://www.imf.org/external/pubs/ft/wp/2002/wp02192.pdf.* See also Perbankan Shariah: Islamic Banking Statistics, Bank Indonesia, December 2002.

6 Bank Indonesia, Blueprint of Islamic Banking Development in Indonesia, *http://www.bi.go.id/bank_indonesia2/utama/publikasi/upload/syariah%20blue%20print-engl.pdf.*

7 Comptroller of the Currency, Administrator National Banking, Office of the Counsel, NY. Interpretative Letter #867, November 1999, 12 USC 34 (7), 12 USC 29; No. 806, December 1997,12 USC (7), 12 USC 371. From bibliography at *http:/www.failaka.com/Failaka/20Research.html.*

8 Sundararajan, op. cit., pp. 16–19.

9 Blueprint, p. 10.

10 I also rely on my visits to Islamic financial institutions in the field and meetings with experts involved in their development. I thank in particular Mr. Adiwarman Karim and his numerous colleagues at Bank Muamalat (especially Mr. Pallas Athene and Asril), and Prof. Dr. Amin Azis, Chairman of Pusat Inkubasi Bisnis Usaha Kecil (Center for Incubating Small Businesses [PINBUK]), which is a project of Yayasan Inkubasi Bisnis Usaha Kecil (Foundation for Incubating Small Businesses [YINBUK]) and a director and leader in other financial institutions suc h as Induk Koperasi Syariah BMT.

11 Blueprint, op. cit.

12 The currency conversion rate used for this paper is 9,000 rupiah (Rp) per US dollar (US$).

13 Dr. Amin Aziz, The Development of Micro Enterprise Institutions in Indonesia: The Case of National Board of Revenue Sharing Micro Enterprise Cooperatives (Induk Koperasi Syariah Bmt, Baitul Maal Wat Tamwil), presented at the Symposium of the APEC Center for Entrepreneurship, Jakarta, August 10, 1999.

14 See footnote 13.

15 See footnote 13.

16 Luca Errico and Mitra Farahbaksh, Islamic Banking: Issues in Prudential Regulations and Supervision, IMF Working Paper, March 1998. Other IMF publications include Nadeem Ul Haque and Abbas Mirakhor, The Design of Instruments for Government Finance in an Islamic Economy, IMF Working Paper, March 1998; and V. Sundarajan, David Marston, and Ghiatt Shabsigh, Monetary Operations and Government Debt Management under Islamic Banking, IMF Working Paper, September 1998. These documents can be accessed at ***http://www.imf.org/external/pubind.htm.***

17 This list differs in minor particulars from the lists in other sources such as a recent IMF study, which mentions in addition: mazar'ah—the counterpart of mudharaba for farming in which the bank provides land or funds and the harvest is shared; musaqat—the traditional counterpart of the musharaka in orchard keeping; direct investment; bai'salam or bai'salaf—purchase with deferred delivery; and joalah—service charge. See V. Sundararajan and Luca Errico, op. cit., pp 21–22.

Index